WHAT OTHERS ARE SAYING ABOUT THIS BOOK

"Congratulations on your outstanding new book *Exceptional Life* . . .looks terrific! You really put it altogether compactly. It will be a great guide for inspired, successful living for all who read it."

--Ed Foreman,
United States Congressman from two different states,
Millionaire by age 26, and Success Expert and Author

"In *Exceptional Life*, Kurt offers a path that will enable you to be transformed by your highest ideals and visions and to live them in practical ways every day of your life. Kurt will show you it is possible and how you can do it. Take the challenge. Wake up. Seize this moment and start to turn your best dreams into reality."

-Joe Brodnicki, President,
Success Navigation Associates

"This book is a roadmap of basic philosophies and practical approaches for a living journey from 'I Will' to 'I Am'.,,,,,with the offering of an " *Exceptional Life* " as the destination."

--Patricia Leonard,
Speaker, Actress and Professional Coach

"Kurt's book is perfectly titled—if you are looking for specific directions on living an *Exceptional Life*, THIS is the road map you've been looking for all your life."

--Bill Karlson, CPC
Author of *Get Top Dollar in a Job You Love*

"Kurt DuNard is a thoughtful and eloquent writer. In reading *Exceptional Life*, I found that, without much effort, I was reflecting on my life's purpose and accomplishments. I have begun the ideas from *Exceptional Life* to enhance my work and relationships."

--Rhonda Borman, MA, MSSW, LCSW,
Author, Speaker, Storyteller

"Kurt DuNard's *Exceptional Life* is a splendid blending of vivid parallels with practical solutions for avoiding the human wastefulness of living the unproductive life. Kurt shares the belief that we come to this earth with unique talents and traits that in themselves are neither good nor bad. However, only when those characteristics of our "hardwiring" are then aligned with higher goals and objectives, do we reach a measure of our true purpose for being. This book is a compass."

--John Bracewell, President
ComposiTEAM™ Leadership System

"This is the book I recommend to people who not only want success but also meaning, happiness and significance."

--Robin Crow, Entertainer,
Author of *Jump and the Net Will Appear*

"Kurt's stories paint vivid pictures with down to earth examples. He takes impressive ground breaking research and presents it in a way that anyone can understand and use to their benefit beginning today."

--Barbara L. Fielder, Speaker,
Author of *I'm Communicating, but...am I being heard?*
and *Motivation in the Workplace*

Exceptional Life

Living the Life You Were Meant to Live

Kurt W. DuNard

CRANE PRESS

Soli Deo Gloria

Crane Press
Post Office. Box 680367
Franklin, TN 37068

For information about special discounts for bulk purchases, please contact Crane Press Special Sales:
1-800-745-6273 or Orders@CranePress.com

Copyright © 2006 by Kurt W. DuNard

All rights reserved. No part of this book may be reproduced or transmitted in any form or by any means, electronic or mechanical, including photocopying, recording or by information storage and retrieval systems, without permission in writing from the author, except by a reviewer who may quote brief passages in review.

First Edition

LIBRARY OF CONGRESS CATALOGING-IN-PUBLICATION DATA
DuNard, Kurt
Exceptional Life: Living the Life You Were Meant to Live/ by Kurt W. DuNard
P.cm.
Includes index
ISBN-13: 978-0-9765838-8-2
ISBN-10: 0-9765838-8-7
1. Successful Living   I. Title.   2. Success   3. Success—Psychological Aspects   4. Self–actualization   5. Life Skills   6. Satisfaction
BF 501-505.D96 2006
158.1 DUN
Library of Congress Control Number: 2005932686

Book Design: William Longspear

Printed in Canada

To my wife,
Joan DuNard
Whose dedication to me, my life and this book made this all possible. She is my best friend.

About the Author

KURT DuNard is an individual that goes for his dreams—no matter how crazy. He has been everything from a high school industrial arts teacher, owner of several businesses, a Vice President at a major brokerage firm, a CEO of a Pacific Northwest head-hunting firm and an organic farmer. While he was busy having life experiences, making mistakes and creating successes, he became knowledgeable on what it really means to live. This knowledge came not just from his own experiences but from a lifetime of study of over five thousand books, tapes and seminars on all aspects of the exceptional life. Kurt is still a student, however, he has decided to share some discoveries that do not appear in those five thousand volumes.

A gifted speaker and writer, Kurt DuNard connects with individuals from all levels of society, culture and backgrounds. Among others, he has advised executives from such organizations as Microsoft, Costco, Weyerhaeuser, Safeco, Nordstrom, and the State of Washington.

Living in Franklin, Tennessee, he offers customized seminars, executive coaching, weekend retreats, keynotes, and on going personal and professional development.

Kurt may be reached at www.DuNard.com.

Preface—Note to the Reader

THERE is an old Chinese curse—*May you live in interesting times.* Well, we are living in interesting times; however, we don't need to look at it as a curse. In fact, it is a blessing. Everything is changing. The world is changing, business is changing and we are changing the most. Opportunities are numerous and exciting. Change is happening at an ever faster accelerating rate and with it, unheard of fantastic lives await the brave adventurer.

There has never been a better time in history for the individual to create a life that is truly exceptional. We have the opportunity to make a difference. Our purpose is easier to live then ever before.

You will read some stories that demonstrate concepts for the exceptional life. I hope you enjoy them and think of your own stories that demonstrate wisdom and truth. I have also included quotations of people who have lived their purpose. Everyone is meant to live an exceptional life. It is up to us to accept the challenge.

There is not enough room in one book to write up every concept, story or new discovery on the Exceptional Life. Therefore I am including ongoing, updated information on the web site: http://www.DuNard.com. You will also find access to a free weekly newsletter on the same site.

Kurt W. DuNard, Franklin, Tennessee

Acknowledgments

MANY people imagine that writing is a lonely solitary activity. This is not always the case. In fact, many people contributed their thoughts, input, encouragement and expertise to making this book better. So you see there is interaction with other people—it is not so lonely. I should mention that thirty years of research went into this book and much of that research was from some of the greatest thinkers of the ages. Although I did not speak to Plato personally, I feel as if I did through his thoughts via the written word. I acknowledge that my thoughts built on many of these original thinkers. I am indebted to them.

Sometimes all we need is a smile and a kind word to keep us going. The following people gave advice, encouragement or actual work on the book. My editor and wife, Joan, made this all possible. Ed Foreman, Jim Collins, Marianne Williamson, the late M. Scott Peck, M. J. Ryan, Dan Poynter and many more gave in one way or another. Thank you.

Any flaws, errors or omissions are mine and mine alone.

Warning–Disclaimer

THE longer I live the more I realize that the "experts" can be right in one year and wrong the next. So I have gotten to the point that I like to do my own thinking. I like to see what all the "experts" are thinking, past and present, and then come up with my own thoughts. No way am I going to take "experts" at face value and then blindly follow them. By following them I might walk right off a cliff.

We should do our own thinking and research when it comes to anything that is important to us. From how we raise a family to our belief in God, we need to think for ourselves and take responsibility for our own decisions. Don't blame your stockbroker if the stock goes down—he or she was only one input of your research and thinking. Don't blame your doctor if you took medication that ruined your heart—he or she was only one input of your research and thinking. Give no man or woman control over your life. Take control and take responsibility. You have the power in you to know what is best for your life. Use that power!

This book is full of suggestions, ideas and truths as I see them. I may not have perfect eyesight. Therefore, some of the ideas in this book could be wrong. Use this book as one input to your research and do your own thinking. By no means should you follow the suggestions in this book blindly.

This book represents my honest beliefs. I do not have a medical degree, a Ph.D. in psychology, or any other number of "expert" credentials. However, one can read several history books and teach the lessons from those books without having a doctorate in history. We have a right to think and a right to publish those thoughts.

And you must do your research and think before following the suggestions in this book. Thus you can take total responsibility for all your life and all your success.

Contents

Chapter 1
I Will—The Most Magical Two Words   1

Chapter 2
Raison D'être —A Life With Purpose   5

Chapter 3
Love—The Key to Everything   28

Chapter 4
Health—Make it Better and Better   49

Chapter 5
Wealth & Prosperity—Cultivate it
and Give it Away   71

Chapter 6
Balanced Goal Planning—Real Freedom   91

Chapter 7
Believers, Agnostics and Atheists
—In Search of Truth   123

Chapter 8
The Genius in All of Us—Mental Growth   147

Chapter 9
Legacy—a Different Kind of Immortality   171

Chapter 10
Living—A Work in Progress   191

Afterword   207

Appendix A
Your Exceptional Life Calendar   209

Index   217

Chapter 1

I Will—The Most Magical Two Words

God gave us the gift of life; it is up to us to give ourselves the gift of living well.
    **--François-Marie Arouet (Voltaire), 1694-1778
       French Enlightenment writer, deist and
                                    philosopher**

Every moment of your life is infinitely creative and the universe is endlessly bountiful. Just put forth a clear enough request, and everything your heart desires must come to you.

   **--Mohandas Karamchand Gandhi, 1869-1948
         Charismatic leader who led India to
      independence from British colonial rule.**

I Will or I Won't

HAVE you ever considered the wonderful descriptive nature of words that label groups of objects? A gaggle of geese, a school of fish, a pride of lions, a bed of clams and pearls of wisdom are just some common examples. Geese gaggle, fish congregate in schools, lions have pride, clams sleep in beds and wisdom has the value of precious pearls. But perhaps we should look at how wisdom is very much like a pearl.

An oyster without its shell is a gourmet's treat. It is also a treat to fish, crabs and starfish. An oyster is a delicate soft animal that, like a turtle, needs its shell for protection. Everyday that oyster must make itself vulnerable to its enemies by opening its shell and feeding by filtering the water for nutrients. As it feeds it can be attacked by all kinds of vicious life with teeth. But it can also be attacked by non-life—a simple grain of sand. For an oyster that grain of sand is like a thorn in its side, which it can't remove. How does the oyster cope with the grain of sand? It puts layer after layer of a smooth beautiful opalescent pearl coating on the grain of sand. The thing that causes the most pain in its life gets coated by beauty. You would think the oyster would become conditioned to stay closed if every time it opened its shell it opened itself to the risk of death and pain. To be fully alive the oyster must open itself to the world in spite of the risks of death and pain. Otherwise, the oyster will starve and die.

But let's look at what happens when it embraces life and the abundance of food in the ocean. It may die and it may receive the pain of sand but it may also thrive, produce other oysters, grow big and produce a pearl of great price. That pearl will be unique, special and a legacy that only that oyster could produce—a gift to the world founded in pain.

Like that oyster, we humans have a choice. Will we open ourselves to the world with the risk of death and pain or will we close ourselves off, take no risks and live a life of poverty without meaning? Do we embrace the world? Do we embrace life and accept the abundance with the problems it has to offer? Pain and suffering, problems and disappointments are our grains of sand. In every problem, in every challenge there is a hidden blessing. For the oyster the blessing in the irritating sand is that it will cause the oyster to grow a pearl. For us, our problems could cause us to build a company, a life, a service to humanity or a long sought after dream.

Either we open up to the world and embrace life or we don't. Open up and take the risks of death and pain for that is the only road to an exceptional life. Sheltering yourself from risks of death and pain is a sure guarantee that you will receive both.

So which is it, will you or won't you go for the exceptional life? The following chapters will help you open

I Will—The Most Magical Two Words

that shell and embrace life. You may have some pain along the way—you also may make some pearls. Congratulations on your first step.

GET ON THE TRAIN!

"Remember, it does not matter the destination, what matters is that you get on the train."
--Paraphrase from The Polar Express, the movie.

Children have the best literature; however, it is usually wasted on them. Most children already know the wisdom—it is the adults who have forgotten.

Perhaps one of the best movies which is full of wisdom is *The Polar Express*. See this movie even if you do not have a child to hold your hand in reassurance. This movie brings home the lessons of risks, faith, wonder, and positive beliefs in our futures. Our world desperately needs these things. Every one of us needs them.

For me the above quote was the crux of the story. The train represented life and our willingness to participate. Even though we do not know the train's destination or our own future, we won't have a life unless we make the commitment to go for the adventure—to step on board.

Both children in the story were reluctant to step on board and almost lost out on the adventure; all because of fear of the unknown. The train waits for nobody. It is our choice to participate in life. We must use our free will and decide to live a life of adventure, challenge and happiness. How many of us have less courage than the children in the above story? How many of us would have just stood in the snow in our pajamas and watched our life disappear down the tracks?

Another way of putting this concept is to say that we must choose to play the game of life. And we must choose to play the cards we have received in the best way possible.

Sometimes those cards are not very good and we would just like to crawl under the table and cry. That would be equivalent to getting off the train. It would be a major mistake. Because the game is not over—the train ride is not finished and anything can happen. It does in *The Polar Express* and it does in real life.

    Just ask Joni Erickson Tada who was paralyzed from the neck down and has become an artist who paints with her mouth and a best selling author. Just ask Wilma Rudolph who suffered Polio and could hardly walk and who became an Olympic champion runner. Just ask Ray Charles, Zubin Mehta, Lance Armstrong, Mother Teresa, and Ludwig Van Beethoven about being dealt bad cards and still staying in the game and on the train to magnificent victory. It is almost as if the bad cards gave them something special. Or perhaps, they were special. Just like you.

    Do we need to know the destination of the train before we get on board? Do we need to know who will win before we are willing to play the game? Go for all your dreams. It does not matter if we succeed in accomplishing them for they may lead to unexpected wonderful adventures. Become a singer, become an artist, start a business, learn a new language, host an exchange student, learn to become a gourmet cook, fall in love, have children, plant a garden, run for office, start a foundation, get on the train!

    Chapter two helps you find the train schedule and a destination map.

Chapter 2

Raison D'être —A Life With Purpose

As far as we can discern, the sole purpose of human existence is to kindle a light of meaning in the darkness of mere being.

**--Carl Jung, 1875 - 1961
Swiss psychiatrist**

The man without a purpose is like a ship without a rudder - waif, a nothing, a no man. Have a purpose in life, and, having it, throw such strength of mind and muscle into your work as God has given you.

**--Thomas Carlyle, 1795 – 1881
Scottish historian and essayist**

Why You Should Make a Life-Plan For Finding Your Reason For Being—Finding Your Life Purpose

SEEK first your raison d'être and life will become much easier. Seek first your raison d'être and life will become intensely meaningful.

Our raison d'être (reason for being) is not to be happy, however, if we find our raison d'être, we will tend to be happy. A company's raison d'être is not to make profits, however, if it finds its raison d'être, profits are sure to come.

What really is a raison d'être or reason for being? It is not something we choose but something we find. It is something that every cell of our bodies confirms with a knowing that can't be refuted. It is why we were created and why a company was created. It is the super longer-term perspective. It is what we think about on our deathbed with either joy or regret.

Michelangelo Buonarroti found it when he created David. Winston Churchill found it when "he mobilized the English language and sent it into battle." Mother Teresa had it when she served the dying in India. But can all of us be a Michelangelo, Churchill or Mother Teresa? We can if we find our raison d'être. When we find it the world opens, we become creative---sometimes we even become geniuses -- roadblocks disappear. AND YOU CAN FIND YOURS.

Even a dog sometimes finds its raison d'être. Some dogs were born to hunt ducks. The owner may buy one as a pet and never take it duck hunting. That dog loves to chase a ball and take it back to the owner. It loves the owner's praise. It especially loves retrieving the ball from the water. These are all activities similar to duck hunting. Like the dog, we have certain things we love to do that may point in the direction of our raison d'être. But we still don't have a concrete idea of our reason for being. This dog may have never seen a duck and may not know that his raison d'être is to hunt ducks. We also may never have been acquainted with exactly what we should be doing. If England had not been attacked, would Churchill have risen to his greatness? The dog, like us, when presented with a chance to fulfill his life's purpose puts every fiber of his being into finding and retrieving those ducks. He is perhaps the happiest he has ever been in his life. One of the most beautiful things to watch is a great dog retrieving. Some, one would swear, can count. Every duck is brought back with enthusiasm, joy and intelligence beyond what one would expect for a dog.

What could we do if we knew beyond a doubt that we were living the life that we were born to live? What passion, what inspiration, what happiness would be our reward? You can reach your full greatness. Knowing the raison d'être will make it easy and inevitable.

ROOSTER

That duck-hunting dog showed us what is meant to find one's purpose in life. If we pay attention to our pets, they can teach us a lot of wisdom. Perhaps that is one reason we have them. A boxer can teach that life is good and let's enjoy it. We can be tired from a hard day at the office and pets can, with the flick of a tail, change all of that and teach us about unconditional love.

If we pay attention---really pay close attention, they can also teach us about courage, responsibility and how to act as humans.

When my wife and I became somewhat successful in Seattle, I said to her; "Joan, you know if we are ever going to do our dreams---now is the time to take the risk and just do them." So we left our successful careers and started Bear Creek Farms in Southern Missouri. This was an organic farm and it went along with our philosophy of health and providing people with the best products possible.

Now as long as we were going to have a farm, we decided to have the whole farming experience. We thought that would be great fun. We bought a flock of chickens. Now you don't have chickens to make money or to save money. You have them just for the experience. To be quite frank, I am surprised that chickens don't cost $20 each in the grocery store. That is what I would be willing to pay if I did not have to kill it, pluck it or clean it.

The rooster is one of the most interesting of all the chickens in the flock. He is fascinating to watch. By the way, most people believe that a rooster is a male chicken. It is true that all roosters are male however not all male chickens are roosters. Only the top male chicken, after fighting his way to the top of the pecking order is classified a rooster. In other words, the rooster is the leader of the flock. Half of the chickens are males but only one is a rooster.

The rooster has one other job besides being romantic with the hens; it is his job to protect all of the flock. He does this by chasing the chickens into their house at dusk. If he did not do this then all the chickens would be dead in the morning. A fox, possum or coyote will eat any chicken left out of the chicken house at night. You see, when a chicken goes to sleep it can hardly wake up and you can go pick up a sleeping chicken with no trouble at all. The problem is, so can a fox. So this rooster chases the chickens into the chicken house and they fly up into rafters or they roost in boxes on the sides of the wall. Hence he makes the chickens go to roost. He is a rooster.

When we came home to the farm one afternoon, there was great commotion in the yard. Dust flying everywhere, chickens running everywhere and dogs barking and running. A pack of dogs were going after all the chickens. A pack of dogs will kill every single chicken, just for the shear pleasure of the hunt and the chase, and not eat one of them. They go crazy with blood and the carnage.

As we came upon the scene we saw an amazing thing happen. At that moment, the rooster ran out and stepped in front of the dogs facing them down. This rooster acted as if he was invulnerable and planned on killing all the dogs. The dogs were so amazed. They also stopped and faced the rooster. Perhaps the dogs wondered if this rooster knew something that they did not. They wondered if it was a new kind of killer rooster. As if from a single signal, the rooster took off and the dogs resumed the chase all toward this one rooster. The rooster ran in the opposite direction of the other chickens. This seemed to give intelligence to the birds and they all made their escape into the chicken house; that place of safety from foxes coyotes and dogs. This rooster gave the dogs a good run but he was no match for the dogs. He gave his life by being ripped apart by several dogs.

This rooster was a hero. It gave its life to save the other chickens and fulfilled its purpose to protect those chickens. I imagine as it died, it felt satisfied that its life had meaning, perhaps more meaning than that of many humans.

What is the wisdom this rooster taught? It taught us about courage, sacrifice, responsibility and fulfilling one's purpose in life. I believe past corporate executives at Enron and other firms could learn from this rooster. They could learn what it means to protect employees and protect shareholders. They could learn about serving others rather than themselves.

Some New Age books suggest that if we go for our bliss then the money will follow. This rooster did not go for its bliss, after all, his death was very painful. But I am sure he felt content that he had given his best while he lived and that he had fulfilled his purpose in life. He had protected the flock at all costs—that was his purpose and that was why he deserved to lead and be the rooster.

When we lie on our deathbed are we going to say; "Is that all there is?" "Why didn't I go for my dreams?" or "Why didn't I find my purpose for living?" Or are we going to say, "Yes, I did take risks and, yes, I did go for it and I did find my purpose." ?

Will we be able to just lay back with complete satisfaction, no matter how great the pain, knowing that we gave it our best shot just like the rooster?

QUESTIONS

If a dog and a rooster can find their raison d'être, I know for a fact that YOU can find your raison d'être. It just takes thinking and questions and thinking and waiting for answers. It also takes a great desire to find one's purpose, to wake up and realize that this life is what we make of it and what we make of it will be exceptional if we can just find our purpose—our raison d'être.

What is life all about anyway? Why are we born, why do we live and why do we die? These are some of the BIG questions. To say the least, I don't think I will give you definitive answers in this chapter. But if I am lucky you may be able to come up with some of the answers for your own individual life.

Are we living for our jobs? That depends--do we do our jobs for a paycheck or for the satisfaction of serving our boss or customers? Are we in business to make a profit or are we in business to serve and keep customers? Is it OK to put into practice certain policies, which will harm the customer but will increase profits? Is it OK to cheat your boss on the expense report so it will increase your take-home pay? These are also BIG questions and they may point you in the direction of your purpose. Is it money at any cost or is it service and integrity?

How about your family and friends? Does your job or money supersede them? Family and friends are really about love and time. Some believe that love = time. No time for family equals no love for family. How do you feel about these statements? Would you give up a dream job for family or would you give up a dream family for a job? How you answer these questions defines your purpose. Ignore these questions and purpose will be hard to find.

It's not what TV does to you, but what it prevents you from doing that is the most destructive thing about it.

--Zig Ziglar
American Author, Motivational Speaker

What is our place in the world? Are we trying to get by or are we trying to make a difference? How do you spend your free time? That tells you what is most important to you in your life. Is all your free time spent in non-quality activities? I am saying "non-quality" by your own definition.

After a night of horrible TV, do you wish you had instead read a great book? These are your definitions—not mine. How do you define yourself? How do you define your purpose? What is your purpose?

Are we victims or are we our own masters? Do we decide how we will spend our free time or do we complain about how there is nothing on TV? Do we start trying to find the answers to who we are and why we are here or just forget about it? I don't honestly believe anybody's raison d'être is to be a couch potato.

Once you find your purpose you will find your happiness and you will find the power, the insight and inspiration to live at your best.

It is indeed profitable to spend the necessary time to find that divine spark that is within each of us. Make a diary of those beliefs that are really important to you and they will lead you to define your purpose.

BULL'S EYE

Let's admit it, life can be a struggle. Sometimes we are in the groove and doing everything perfectly and then other times we just miss the mark and nothing seems to go right. At those times we may feel the sting of judgment from others.

I don't know about you, but I get pretty uncomfortable when the preacher goes to the pulpit and says: "You are all sinners—REPENT!!!" I think of sinners as slash murderers, thieves, liars and cheats and I know with a certainty that I am not one of those. Maybe the preacher is talking to several people in the back rows. Should I trust those people?

The word sin is translated from the word *hamartia*. It literally means a miss. It is an archery term and it means to miss the bull's eye of the target. Have we all been hitting bull's eyes every day when it comes to living our life purpose? My belief is that the real sin comes when we don't find our life purpose or our raison d'être and we waste our lives doing something that is unfulfilling, unrewarding and uninspiring. It is as if God said: "I gave you life to fulfill a unique mission--raison d'être and I want you to accomplish that mission." And the uninformed say: "No thanks—we don't have time to think about it." Perhaps that is the only thing worth thinking about.

Think about the uniqueness of every individual. We were all given different fingerprints. No two are alike and law enforcement has been identifying people by their fingerprints for over a hundred years. Each and every voice is completely different—again this fact is used for security systems. Each retina of our eyes is also completely unique from any other person's retina. Eye scans are also being used by security systems. No two person's DNA is exactly alike. Even identical twins have different fingerprints, voices, retinas, and DNA. If we are all as different as a snowflake, doesn't it make sense that we could all have different life purposes, different reasons for being, a different raison d'être? Isn't our real challenge to find the center of the target, to find our individual purpose in life and then to shoot for the bull's eye?

No matter what our religion, faith or lack there of, it is our responsibility to find how we can reach our best selves. We must live a life where our best potential is reached. We must live a life where our unique purpose blooms and makes the world a better place. Only you can find the center of the target. Only you can find your life purpose. That is what this chapter is all about.

GENIUS AND LIFE PURPOSE

Perhaps we are not consumed with our raison d'être because we are not thinking enough or are not using enough of our brains. We have never given serious thought to what exactly is our purpose.

Experts say that we only use 5% of our brains. Did you ever wonder what the other 95% was for? Just think if you could use 6% or 7%----or 100%. If you could, you would be a

Raison D'être — A Life With Purpose

genius compared to everyone else. Well, you can and it is easy. Your brain is just waiting for you to tap into this power. I am going to prove it to you if you have the courage to perform an experiment.

It is my contention that those people whom we consider to be geniuses are only using more of their brains. Some only stumbled onto this secret by accident. I am going to help you with that secret.

The 95% of the brain that is not used is a part of the brain that cannot be used in the same way as our conscious brain (5% part). In addition to making our heart, lungs and everything else in our body work on automatic, that 95% part of the brain also contains our subconscious. To be a genius, one must work with the subconscious. This is a natural, easy thing to do. We were born to use our subconscious; it is only our Western scientific culture that has looked askance at this practice by romanticizing the conscious/logic side of the brain. It is indeed ironic that many of the heroes of science are those who *did* use their subconscious. We called them geniuses when really they were only thinking in unorthodox ways.

When Albert Einstein was in his twenties, one sunny day he lay in the grass and while half awake and half asleep watched a dust particle glide on a sunbeam. His imagination took off and he imagined what would happen if that particle traveled throughout the universe. He tapped into his subconscious and came up with the Theory of Relativity.

Thomas Alva Edison wanted to be the greatest inventor that ever lived. He would intentionally put himself into that same mental state that Einstein found so conducive to thought. He would recline in a chair with steel ball bearings in each outstretched hand. As he became half awake and half asleep he would tap into his subconscious mind. When he became too relaxed, he would drop the ball bearings into metal pie pans and wake up.

At this point, he immediately wrote down his great ideas. This was crucial as ideas that come in sleep or during half-awake states are more slippery than a fish and will be soon forgotten. Edison did become one of the greatest inventors of all time. The same genius that made Edison great is available to you; however, it is only available if you have the courage to explore a part of yourself that is unfamiliar.

    Nikola Tesla, an American immigrant, was perhaps the greatest inventor that ever lived. I am sure Edison would disagree, however, Tesla is the reason we have AC current, radio (no Marconi did not invent radio as many text books still teach. His patents were upheld and proven to predate Marconi in a 1975 Supreme Court ruling), cell phones and other inventions and discoveries that are so far advanced that we still do not know their implications. Tesla would think and dream about each invention in every detail. You could almost say that he would do a computer simulation of the invention in his head. He would find design flaws and then re-think about how to correct those flaws and make the invention work. He was one of the only inventors of the late 1800's early 1900's who could think about an invention and then build a perfect working model every time. He was definitely using much more than 5% of his brain.

    Would you like to become a genius by tomorrow morning? Let's try an experiment, if you have the courage to start living an exceptional life. I want you to start keeping a diary of inspired subconscious thoughts, similar to Edison. Keep this diary by your bed with a pen ready to write. Before going to bed quiet your mind and look at the biggest challenges you are now facing. Date and write your questions in the diary. Write out question whose answers will change your life. Start with specific questions on the problems of your life or use some of the following general questions such as:

What is important for me to know now?

What is the most important thing I could do now to find my dream job?

What would be my dream job?

What must I do now to become healthy?

How can I find love in my life?

What is my purpose in life?

How can I make my life meaningful?

What is the most important thing I can do now for my career?

The important thing when writing down these questions is that you must really desire answers. You must be emotionally enthusiastic about the outcome. You must also believe that your subconscious will give you answers. It will! Also keep the diary with you all day. Sometimes the answers come during weird times.

This is your experiment:

- ❖ Write down several important questions just before bedtime.

- ❖ Expect an incredible answer in the middle of the night or in the morning or later in the day. Just know that if you ask—you will receive.

- ❖ As soon as you get the answer, write it down.

❖ Act on the answer and write down the results. I believe you will find them to be amazingly positive. It is important to act on the answers because as you do you will become more powerful at receiving incredible information.

❖ Continue with this process for the rest of your life.

LEARNED HELPLESSNESS

Some of us are stuck and we need help getting unstuck. What is amazing is that it can be simple if we understand the psychology behind our helplessness.

Psychologist Dr. Martin Seligman did some amazing research, which I believe could direct us to the cure of self-sabotage. Have you ever given up on a diet? Has your exercise program been forgotten? Do you put your dreams on hold for invalid petty reasons? If you are single, have you stopped looking for the perfect spouse? These are all self-sabotaging behaviors which all of us have had to struggle with from time to time. Sometimes we just give up. Dr. Seligman's research points to a cure. So if you would like to get in perfect shape and would like to find the love of your life and would like to live your dreams then read on.

Dr. Seligman did scientific laboratory research using dogs. His findings aimed in the direction of possible reasons why people may get stuck and why they may just give up---why they become helpless. What is more important is his research also gives possibilities of how one can get un-stuck and start on the road to success.

He took dogs and placed them in a chamber and made their life continuously unpleasant by electrifying the floor such that it would always give a mild shock. These dogs did everything to escape the shock. They ran, they jumped, and they howled and wriggled. Nothing worked and they were still shocked. They learned helplessness. They learned the attitude of: What's the use? Why try? They believed that they were helpless to the continuous shock. They were no longer naïve--- they were realistic. They believed the world was bad and that nothing they could do would change their situation.

Dr. Seligman then did a second experiment. He made it possible for the dogs to succeed. He created a barrier in the middle of the chamber which, if jumped over, the dogs would escape the shock. He brought in new dogs and they quickly found the barrier and escaped. When he brought in the "old" dogs, they ran around quickly reverting to their learned "realistic" attitude and lay down in the corner and accepted a bad life of shocks.

Dr. Seligman wondered if these "old" dogs could learn the new tricks of escaping the shocks. He would help the dogs find the barrier and help them jump over it to success. Most did not register the new information. In fact, most ignored success. He had to help each dog between 25 and 200 times over the barrier before it finally got it and registered the new information. These dogs believed in failure and helplessness. Even though there was overwhelming evidence to the contrary they chose to be helpless time after time after time.

Fortunately we are not dogs. We are humans with a higher level of critical thinking. However, if we do not use this critical thinking then we can start acting like those "old" dogs. When we put our life on "automatic" we put our thinking on automatic. Those "old" dogs learned that they could not have success under the first experiment. Their automatic thinking made them believe this in spite of the new evidence of the second experiment. They continued to give up for another 25-200 times before they changed their thinking.

We can also be programmed to think we can't have success and we can't find our purpose. After a while we can give up like the dogs. Here are some ways to avoid this tragedy.

Constantly look for evidence that success is possible. Are other people succeeding under worse conditions? Are other people finding their reason for being and finding happiness?

Keep your attitude positive so that you will not give up. Remember Winston Churchill when it looked like England would perish. He never gave in.

Imagine and visualize success and living your life purpose. Your subconscious can't tell the difference between imagined and actual success. Athletes imagining perfect free-throws twenty minutes a day improved their performance as much as the ones who did the actual practice.

Celebrate small victories. It will convince you that the big ones are possible. Weight Watchers and Toastmasters International use this method to help their members stay on the program. This will work for you.

People who believe in a Higher Being and prayer believe that they will be saved by super natural powers. Whether it is true or not, the fact that they believe this gives them a psychological advantage over those that do not. These people never become like the "old" dogs because they keep trying and trying and trying and hoping for intervention.

Men and woman who have been the most admired through the ages were often admired for succeeding under overwhelming conditions, persisting even after great failure and still finding a way to succeed. Mother Teresa's own order refused her request to help the poor and dying of India five times before they agreed to let her go. And then they only agreed to let her go if she would go with **NO MONEY**. Her success and life purpose was one that spread to the world. In another example, a few farmers decided to take on the largest military industrial complex in the world and won. We know them better as our founding fathers.

What are we doing to coax our subconscious to never give up? The world is our oyster. Is it going to take 25-200 pieces of evidence before we start believing in our own success?

HAPPINESS OR RAISON D'ÊTRE AND QUOTATIONS

When we look at advertising and commercials we would almost think that our life purpose is to consume, find pleasure and avoid pain. But there are greater things in life than only caring about one's self and one's pleasures. Our raison d'être or our reason for being is one of those things. In fact, many people are quite willing to go through pain, misery and even death to accomplish their raison d'être. When we have our real raison d'être right in front of our face and we are intensely focused on that life purpose then we find how unimportant and trivial are those things that are advertised and in commercials. Our true-life priorities come sharply into focus and we never give in.

Winston Churchill, who did <u>not</u> say: "Never, never, never, never give up."

He did in fact say:

Never give in—never, never, never, never, in nothing great or small, large or petty, never give in except to convictions of honour and good sense. Never yield to the force; never yield to the apparently overwhelming might of the enemy.

This is the entire speech that Sir Winston Churchill gave in 1941 to the Harrow School. He gave this small speech and walked off the stage. This speech made him famous for something he never said.

I am sure Churchill found humor in this fact for he was a devotee to quotation books. He would spend many an evening just paging though these books finding wisdom with each blink of the eye. Churchill felt that quotation books gave clues to the great authors one should read. Interesting quotations meant for him interesting authors and he would search out their books.

Of course the quotations that Churchill liked the most told him a lot about himself. It helped him to know with crystal clarity exactly what was important to him. This gave him certainty when it came to finding his purpose in life.

Recently a beautiful quotation has been attributed to Nelson Mandela's 1994 Inauguration Speech. Nelson Mandela not only did not say this quotation in his Inauguration Speech, he did not say it in any published speech in 1994. However, very reputable publications still circulate this misinformation. The person who is actually the author of the following quotation is Marianne Williamson.

Here is her quotation:

Our deepest fear is not that we are inadequate. Our deepest fear is that we are powerful beyond measure. It is our light, not our darkness that most frightens us. We ask ourselves, 'Who am I to be brilliant, gorgeous, talented, fabulous? Actually, who are you not to be? You are a child of God. Your playing small does not serve the world. There is nothing enlightened about shrinking so that other people won't feel insecure around you. We are all meant to shine, as children do. We were born to make manifest the glory of God that is within us. It is not just in some of us; it is in everyone.

And as we let our own light shine, we unconsciously give other people permission to do the same. As we are liberated from our own fear, our presence automatically liberates others.

--Marianne Williamson, author of A Return to Love

Does that quotation give you hope? Buy a quotation book today and make it part of your study and search for values and your raison d'être. Use it as a tool to grow and a tool to find those lights that will lead you to your Promised Land. A quotation book is a passport to the best thoughts of all time but it is also a passport to finding exactly what we believe. It teaches us about ourselves. Remember always keep your diary or journal close at hand so you can make notes and comments about YOUR beliefs.

Making a Raison d'être Plan

Let's make an assumption for the sake of argument. Let's assume that a creator, an infinite intelligence, a God or some higher power did create each of us for some specific purpose. Let's also assume that our highest good would come only if we could discover that purpose and live it with all our might. What would the best method be for finding our raison d'être with complete inner knowing and confidence?

Recognize that our purpose in life is not necessarily our job. Although some people are fortunate enough to have their job and their raison d'être complement each other. Finding one's calling is different from finding a good job. One you love and would do for free. The other is OK but it does not give the same satisfaction.

What you are good at is not always something you want to do for the rest of your life. However, what you are good at gives clues to finding your purpose.

If our maker wants us to do a specific mission in life, wouldn't it make sense that we would be given certain gifts and tools to accomplish that mission? That duck-hunting dog talked about earlier was given the gifts of swimming, retrieving and the intelligence to find all the ducks. The rooster was given the gift of courage, self-sacrifice, and the intelligence to lead the dogs away from the other chickens. You have also been given specific gifts. A combination of your gifts creates a catalyst for a unique mission that only you will be able to accomplish. It is our job to solve the biggest riddle of our lives. What is our raison d'être? Once we have the answer then we must dedicate our lives to this purpose.

> ❖ In your journal list all your gifts and talents. If you want an even greater knowledge of your gifts and talents then take a formal assessment such as the Johnson O'Connor or many others. If, for instance, they say that you could be an accountant then being an accountant could be a job or a purpose in life. What we need to ask ourselves is how could a person, who in this instance would make a good accountant, find a meaningful course in life, a raison d'être that would require accountant like gifts? It may not be as an accountant that you were meant to serve, however, you may need to have accountant like gifts to serve in another position. Are you using all your gifts right now? What unique set of circumstances would require the use of all your gifts? Use your journal.

So we are assuming we are given gifts that will help us be successful accomplishing our purpose. What about knowledge and experience? It is my contention that everything we learn, read and experience is changing us into the unique person that could help the world in unbelievable ways. If a person is fired, divorced, deals with a life threatening illness or has to work with the pain of being overweight then that person could learn compassion for those people who are dealing with these issues. When we go through hard times we tend to be more compassionate toward others going through similar hard times. All experience changes us making us uniquely qualified for our raison d'être. What we learn in school and especially what we learn from books and self-study also changes us. To read a thousand books gives us a similar experience to having lived a thousand lives. Your subconscious can't tell the difference between an imagined life and an actual life. We become even more powerful and uniquely qualified to pursue our raison d'être. What have you learned through your life of study that makes you uniquely qualified for your purpose in life?

- ❖ List the important experiences in your life. How did they affect you? How are you a different person as a result of that experience and how is that a positive to others?
- ❖ List major areas of knowledge that may point to your purpose in life. How can this knowledge help you in your raison d'être?

There is no wasted experience in life—all can be used. All learning has value--none is wasted. We may think that basket-weaving course we took at summer camp is of no value and was a waste, however our raison d'être could take us to some primitive people on an isolated island in the South Pacific and it is that basket-weaving knowledge that may open the minds of the people to accepting you as a good person. Our experiences and learning work in mysterious ways to further our success and point to our reason for being.

Find your heroes and you find yourself

- ❖ In your journal list a hundred people you respect, love and judge to be superior people. These can be people you personally know, living or dead, people from history or even people that never lived except in fictional books or plays. Once you have your list, write the main reason you admire each person. You will notice that a pattern forms of the traits you most admire in people. Your heroes are really a reflection of your higher self. These are people who reflect back to you the kind of individual you could become. Does that excite you? What if your raison d'être made you into the kind of person you most admire? Would that give you enough energy to do almost anything?

What will people say about you once you are gone?

❖ Again write in your journal. In this exercise you are trying to find what is of ultimate value in your life. Imagine that you have lived your raison d'être and now your soul is privileged to overhear what is said at your funeral. Remember you have lived your life letting your purpose drive your actions. Also, remember that the traits of the heroes above could be your traits. Write your own eulogy as you hope that it will be written. Write what friends, family and business associates say about you. Let your imagination really explore everyone even the grocery clerk at the market. I would imagine that the preacher did not say that you had the biggest house in town or the fastest car. I think you will find that the main focus tends toward those things you did that affected other people. This exercise will let you know what you really think is important. It also points in the direction of your raison d'être.

Act as if you know your purpose in life

❖ Imagine that someone has asked you to describe your raison d'être. Write down a description in as much detail as possible. What is your life like? Describe a day in the life of yourself. Where do you live? What kind of people are you working with or are you working with people? Describe your home and your place of work. Describe what you are doing that is so exciting. What kind of food do you eat? How are you dressed? Do you use all the modern technology like computers to amplify your efforts? Are you famous or are you accomplishing your work anonymously? Have people seen your vision and are you receiving both help and money to accomplish that vision? Are there skills that you are learning so you can pursue your purpose? Do you need to know a foreign language? Are you researching at the library and over the Internet to find answers for your vision? How does it feel to work with others? Describe your joys. Describe your challenges. Who are your allies? Who are your enemies and how can you make them your allies? How will the world be different because you lived your raison d'être?

A word of caution

If we were born to live a certain kind of life—a life with a well defined purpose or to live our raison d'être, then it is only logical to believe that it is possible to succeed at living that special life. A bird is meant to fly but I'll bet he has plenty of fear just before he is pushed from the nest. In fact, if he were like many people, he would never leave the nest just to be safe. These people fall into a trap of fear, doubt and misconceptions that causes them to give up on their dreams and live a life of regret and misery. Here are common fears and misconceptions that keep many from soaring like eagles:

❖ Fearing that money and passion do not go together. Fearing that if we go for what we really care about we will end up broke. The opposite is true. When we have passion for what we are doing, we put incredible energy and creativity into our dream. This is what it takes to become world class and exceptional. These people tend to be well rewarded.

❖ Fear that once we decide to go for our raison d'être there will be no turning back and all future possibilities will be limited. Untrue! It will give you more options because you have more experience and vision. Also, you can always change your mind when you have better, newer information. Remember there are no wasted experiences and all experiences lead to your purpose.

❖ Fear of not being able to clearly see the future and see definable goals. Whether you go for your purpose in life or you don't go for your purpose you will not be able to foresee the future. Goals are only approximates, best guesses and, although important, not mandatory for starting a better life. Sometimes it is just better to start and know that the future and goals will reveal themselves when appropriate.

The best-laid plans of mice and men often go awry.
--Robert Burns, 1759-1796 Scottish Poet

❖ A fear that everyone you know will stop loving you because you will change and become a different person. This is unlikely and perhaps an excuse for not going for your purpose in life. It is more likely that more people will like and love you than before because you are your authentic self. It is when we try to change ourselves to fit other's expectations that we end up having people treat us with indifference and we become miserable because we don't even love ourselves. When we become our authentic self we move from being like an ordinary piece of chocolate to becoming an intensely flavored piece of the best Swiss chocolate you ever tasted. If you love chocolate you will love this person more intensely. If you dislike chocolate then you will dislike this person more intensely. Some people don't like chocolate. That does not mean we should try to be a different flavor just for their sakes.

❖ The belief and misconception that we can't begin our life until we have a precise correct answer that tells us exactly what we must do. The idea that if we don't know our raison d'être then we can't begin. UNTRUE! Using your journal and keeping you eyes and ears wide open, you can find the answers by living, by thinking, by journaling, by dreaming, by meditating, by praying, and by making mistakes. The important thing is to start.

Chapter 3

Love—The Key to Everything

A new commandment I give unto you, That ye love one another...
*--***John 13:34**

There is the same difference in a person before and after he is in love as there is in an unlighted lamp and one that is burning. The lamp was there and it was a good lamp, but now it is shedding light too, and that is its real function.
---Vincent Van Gogh, 1853-1890
Dutch Painter

Why You Should Make a Life-Plan For Love

AS I write this chapter, it is February 14th—Valentine's Day, that holiday when we show the love of our life that we love them or we sit at home in pain because we are alone. We may send a card, flowers or take them to dinner but the main importance of this holiday is to *show someone else* that we really love them. Both men and women long to be told and shown that they are loved.

Before we go any further let's define what we mean by "love." Most people like to define love as a feeling or caring for someone else. This is not enough. For there to be real love those feelings must cause the person to take a positive action for the other person. The ideas and feelings of caring must precipitate a loving action. Without action it is only a daydream. Saying to your son that you will "try" to make his game is not love. Love is when you show up at the game even though an unfinished report is waiting on your office desk. Love is an action word that shows someone else that we care. It shows that we have compassion, trust and feelings of doing good for the other person. It is when we think of the other person in terms of what we can do for them instead of what they can do for us. Words of love can be a pretense but actions of love and real caring are hard to fake. Ending a phone call with "I love you" in hopes of making the other person say "I love you too" is not love if it is manipulative. So with this definition, we are not talking about sex. However, hopefully, we marry and make love with the one we love. If we take sex out of the definition then it is possible to love almost anyone.

Do we really need love in our lives? Are we not rugged individualists with no need of anyone else? If we need love then does not that need make us weak? We need love like we need air, water and food. We will become weak if we do not get love. You have heard of people who have died of a broken heart. Broken hearts have been claimed for thousands of years. Only recently have scientists confirmed that people's hearts can stop through emotions even with a completely healthy heart. Few understand the importance of love and few plan their life so that it will be filled with love.

When a baby is born it MUST receive love or it will die. This is very well known within the scientific community and as a result nurses hold babies, talk to babies and, in effect, love the new born babies. Perhaps babies are not the only people who die when they are not loved. Would the elderly live longer if they were not put into the equivalent of solitary confinement? Their friends have died, their family may have abandoned them and they could be sick and unpleasant to be around. They are starved for love and could be dying from that lack of the same. Don't let this happen to you!

Here is the great secret of the ages:

The only thing people really want is to be loved. Give enough people the love they want and you will have all the love you want.

MOTHER TERESA

Perhaps one of the greatest experts on the subject of love was Mother Teresa. Her missions to help the poor and dying were as much for the sisters and brothers of the missions as they were for the indigent and suffering. But what most people don't understand is that they were not just about helping the suffering they were primarily about giving love.

A story is told how an older wealthy man came to see Mother Teresa. In frustration, he told her how his sons and daughters were all living in other parts of the world—that he and his wife never saw them. He said: "I am half blind, my wife is going mental and all we want is to talk with someone." They were rich in material goods but poor in their love life. They were dying from a lack of love just as surely as a newborn baby will die if it is not loved. They did not even have someone with whom to talk. Mother Teresa sent a sister just as if this couple were poor and homeless for surely they were poor in spirit and poor in love.

Many are surprised to find out that the Mother Teresa's missions are not just located in India. They are all over the world including the United States. We have one in New York, Detroit, St Louis and Los Angeles. Why would we need them when we are such a rich country? Could it be because we are poor in spirit and poor in love?

Mother Teresa said that the poor and dying were gifts from God. These people had lost everything, including their health, and now all they had to offer was love. When her sisters and brothers brought them to the mission and gave them compassion, tenderness, and a loving attitude, these people would promptly reciprocate with angelic smiles and true hearts of love. Reporters and visitors would often comment about the euphoric happiness that was displayed by the hard working missionaries. The place had a feeling of holiness just because of all the love that was being given and taken and given and taken. That older, wealthy man who was dying from a lack of love only needed to give love to the poor and dying and he would have had more love than he could handle.

Mother Teresa thought the United States was rich materially but very poor spiritually. She felt, like Leo Buscaglia, that we did not love one another enough. She is right!

How can we plan a life that will be full of love and where we will never end up like that poor wealthy couple? *What you want more of you must give away.* In other words, we must give love if we want to get love. The only problem is that any love we give must have no strings attached. Love must be given with no expectation of any being returned. Otherwise, it is insincere. It must be given with a true heart.

There is an excellent movie that every family should go and see. I believe it will someday become a classic like other movies that teach great wisdom. It is called *Uncle Nino*. This movie has great values and, most importantly, promotes the idea of loving one another. Uncle Nino comes from Italy to visit his ladder climbing, high-pressure job nephew and his family in America. Nino brings the love from the old country to a family that is about to explode from poor values and the American society. It is a wonderful contrast of our culture and a culture that is full of love. He shows them what love really means. If only we could all adopt Uncle Nino's philosophy on life. America would be a better place—a more joyful place.

We should tell one another that we care and that we hold the other in our heart. We should not limit this to family only. We should tell neighbors, coworkers and sometimes even strangers that we care. But that is not good enough. If we really care, then that love will be manifested with the fruit of action. We will do something for the other person that will improve that other person's life. We will take off work early to go to our son's soccer game. We will insist on taking time to eat dinner with the family so that we can know what is going on in each member's life. We will talk to our neighbors and introduce ourselves to them. If their interest is gardening then we will ask about it and contribute to their interests. We will be interested in our coworkers and see how we can help their careers. And we may smile at an ugly fat stranger just to give some love. In short, we will love them. We will do for him or her that which we wish someone would do for us. We will think about how to give love instead of how to get love.

TO FEEL LOVED

When was the last time you really felt loved? Was it that time when your spouse wanted your opinion about their job? Or when your child wanted help with his or her math? Or when your employer was really interested in your ideas about the new project? Was the last time you really felt loved when you really felt needed? Was it when your ideas were valued? When you were valued?

It is my contention that when we value people for their ideas, we are valuing them for themselves and giving them love. Asking for another's thoughts is perhaps the most intimate thing we can request. It is also the action that builds community and teams.

One of the main complaints of couples getting a divorce is that they never talk anymore. Teenagers and parents notice that there is a strain in relations when family dialog gets to only a few minutes a day. Factory workers complain that the boss wants them to leave their brain at home and only do the job. On the other hand, the neighbor who wants to talk seems to be our best neighbor.

Most legendary companies had one thing in common. They respected people, respected employees, respected customers, shareholders, and all stakeholders. That respect was really a form of love. The action came when they wanted to know what these people thought. In other words, they loved them—they valued them. In return, the stakeholders felt valued and gave their all to support the company. When the restaurant manager asks each guest about the quality of service and food, that guest feels valued and loved. He or she is more likely to return and recommend the restaurant.

Ask your employees what they think or the best will leave. Ask your customers what they think or many will leave. Talk with your spouse. Talk with your children—ask them what they are doing in their lives. Talk with your aging parents. If you don't, you may lose them in fact or at least lose them emotionally. Aging parents also need to have a genuine interest in their grown children's lives. Ask about their complicated high-tech jobs even though you do not understand them.

Ask your employees--What is it that I really need to know to improve this company?

Ask your boss—What is the most important part of my job in which you want me to focus the greatest amount of energy?

Ask your customer—What do I need to do to make my business serve you better?

Ask your family—How is your life going? What are your joys? What are your concerns? What are your dreams?

Ask these questions and you will be amazed how the world seems to change.

We never know how far a smile or a kind word will resonate with a person and in turn with their family and eventually on down through the generations. They say that child abuse is passed on from generation to generation. Love is also passed on from generation to generation.

People are so starved for love that some are willing to commit suicide if they must continue to live in the pain. Why is love in so short a supply? Perhaps because we have been taught to not talk to strangers and to only give love to family and a few friends. That is crazy and is one of the main causes of ruined lives, loneliness and depression. One could say this craziness causes craziness. So how should we give love? How do we make people feel loved? How can you tell when an organization is on the love track?

Let me tell you about my professor who was on the love track and who inspired his students to do better.

Professor Bent

When are you at your best? When do you do your best work? When are you the most creative? Aren't you amazed at how much work you can get done just before a vacation? Why is that? Have you noticed you do great work for those you love or at least like a little? Grouchy threatening managers do not get the best work out of their employees.

When I attended the University of Missouri I was required to take a chemistry course as one of my general education requirements. To be quite frank, science is not one of my favorite subjects. But when I took chemistry under Professor Bent, it became one of my favorite subjects. This man loved his students and we loved him back. We were happy in his lectures, in his labs, and, believe it or not, during his tests. He put his all into teaching and we put our all into learning. What made us excel? Zig Ziglar says "People really don't care how much you know until they know how much you care." Dr. Bent really cared–he loved us. We were happy, content and joyful. We excelled because we loved Professor Bent and wanted to do well for him. Don't students do better for teachers they love?

What does this have to do with business or any human relationship? Everything! If your family, employees, customers, management, stockholders or suppliers are not happy, content and joyful then it is possible that they are not giving you their best. To put it another way, if you and everyone around you are not having a blast, then profits could be much, much higher. Do you care about people or do you care about what they can do for you? Believe me, the employees or students know which way you really feel and they will perform accordingly. Those companies that put into practice "love" programs just to get more production out of their people will see it backfire. You can't give fake love for higher productivity. The love has to be real.

Business, marriage and relationships do not have to be run like a war. As we know "War is Hell," why would anyone want to work or be in Hell? Managing people like you are at war brings on a war mentality. A war mentality makes it ok to lie, cheat or steal. We have seen a lot of this with many of the corporate scandals in recent years. Ultimately, it even allows murder, as some would argue that is what war profiteering is all about. Profits through theft, injustice and hate all cause misery, destruction, broken marriages, layoffs and Hell. It is what puts stress in business and on families. Perhaps it is not a good idea to get our business leaders from the military unless they agree to make love in business and not war.

Setting up a family or business environment to have a blast, to have fun, to have contentment and joy will set up an environment of trust and build up social capital. Like Professor Bent you will find amazing results from your family, customers, employees and all stakeholders. They will do things to help you and your company that are unbelievable. The most amazing thing of all, though, is that you will change and become joyful too. Your family is happier and next quarter's numbers seem to take care of themselves. Your worry is no longer needed. All you need to do is manage your joy.

COMPASSIONATE IRIS

The quality of mercy in not strained,
It droppeth as the gentle rain from heaven
Upon the place beneath. It is twice blest;
It blesseth him that gives and him that takes.
'Tis mightiest in the mightiest. It becomes
The thronèd monarch better than his crown.
His scepter shows the force of temporal power,
The attribute to awe and majesty
Wherein doth sit the dread and fear of kings.
But mercy is above the sceptered sway,
It is enthronèd in the hearts of kings,
It is an attribute to God himself,
And earthly power doth then show likest God's
When mercy seasons justice.

--The Merchant of Venice
William Shakespeare, 1554-1616
English Playwright

When I was in grade school I lived next door to a kind old lady. As I get to be close to her age my perspective has changed. She was probably a kind young lady.

With no one to play with and being an imaginative kid, I saw her beautiful iris garden as not just flowers but as flowers amongst unusual leaves. To a young boy those leaves look like handy swords to pick. In my imagination, I could pick an iris leaf and instantly be on the deck of a pirate ship fighting the scallywags. I don't think my kind old neighbor could see my vision.

At first, my parents told me not to pick the leaves. But they were so tempting and so much fun. My neighbor did not have to worry about dogs or rabbits—Kurt brought more than enough destruction.

By most people's codes of justice I deserved to be punished. I deserved to be spanked, grounded or humiliated. That did not happen. Instead I was loved.

This kind old lady, in a way, adopted me. She bought me a subscription to a children's magazine, she had me and my brother and sisters over for a party and, most importantly, she did something I never expected. One day I came home from school and I found my mother and Mrs. Wright in my back yard digging. My kind old lady was giving me some of her irises to start my own iris garden. Unbelievable, no hate, no resentment, only love. This impressed me a great deal. My new and very own iris garden was something I loved. They made it completely clear that it was my garden and not my mother's. My neighbor lady and I became best friends and she would often come over to see if I wanted to tour her full magnificent garden. She would tell me all about all the flowers.

To this day, I love gardens because they represent love and compassion when punishment was more deserved. The iris is my favorite flower and every home I have owned had an iris garden. Even the love of my life and wife of over thirty years has the middle name Iris. I always felt she had to be the one if she had Iris in her name.

Look at how this kind neighbor took something that was potentially negative and turned it into a lesson for a little boy that lasted a lifetime. If we give compassion and love instead of punishment and hate then the world will become a paradise. As a wise man once said: "Love your enemies." I wonder if war would be impossible if we followed this advice?

LOVE DENIED AND ITS ANTIDOTE

All children deserve and need love.

There is an ugly little secret that is not talked about in polite company. Some parents do not love their children. In fact, some parents hate their children. This is more common than most would admit. The children won't admit it for they are hoping against hope that somehow they will be able to earn their parents love. The parents won't admit it because society would condemn them as bad parents. Generally, these parents had children for the wrong reasons. They had them not so they would have children to love but so they would have children that would love them. In other words, they had children to fulfill their own needs for love with no thought of returning that love. Most children worship their parents almost as gods until the age of twelve. At that age the child starts thinking in deeper terms and starts becoming an adult. He or she starts seeing that the parents are not Gods and starts wondering why love is being withheld and why they are starting to be treated as parasites or liabilities. Without being worshiped as gods these parents feel betrayed and start hating their children. They think: "Why can't my children be more grateful? After all I gave them life, I made them."

    What does withheld love do to the children of these love- draining parents? Most of these children end up having low self-esteem. They feel unlovable and unworthy. Some will spend their lives in counseling. Others will spend their lives trying to get their parents to love them in any way possible. They will never succeed for these parents are incapable of love.

    Many of these children upon maturity can, also, have a tendency to be incapable of love and will be looking for a spouse or for his or her own children to fill this void. They can be like their parents. They may look for a spouse that will love them instead of a spouse that they can love. This can lead to divorce. They may have children so that they will have children to love them rather than to have children to love. If this happens then we see the whole process started again. This can happen to children of unloving parents but it does not have to happen.

    Denying or withholding love from one's children is perhaps some of the most damaging, grievous child abuse possible. It can destroy the child's life, and if the parent is long lived, it will continue until the son or daughter is in his or her 50's, 60's or 70's. It will not stop. That is why when we hear about the son or daughter who will not visit his mother or father in the retirement home we should not be quick to judge. That son or daughter may just be avoiding more abuse.

How can these children regain their lives? What is the antidote for love denied? The antidote is to give love to as many people as possible. Giving love is the best way to create love in your life. We must give away that which we want.

And in the end, the love you take is equal to the love you make.
--The Beatles

But there is always a hollow place in the heart for those who did not receive a parent's love. It seems that no other love will replace that longed for parental love. It is really our first love. If the pain persists then I recommend thinking about the following: Your parents did not give you life and they did not make you. God gave you life and God made you. Your parents were only vessels for God's work. You are a child of God and God loves you. God is your real mother and father. You do not need your parent's love as you have God's love.

THE FIRST GRADE TEACHER

The parents have the greatest impact on our self-esteem, however teachers can also wield a powerful club or a powerful helping hand.

When I started kindergarten, my family had just moved to Missouri from the State of Washington. It was a big move to a part of the country that spoke a different kind of English. We were new kids in the school and we sounded funny. Making friends was going to be a challenge. However, I did ok and I loved my kindergarten teacher. She loved her students. In fact, I told my parents that I would someday marry a woman that had her hair in a ponytail just like my teacher. I got good reports and my parents were told I would do well in first grade.

My older brother and sister are fraternal twins. You should have seen them. For them English was a second language as they started with their own private language that they invented. Can you imagine the intelligence it takes to invent your own language? Although they were not identical twins they were very close and one would swear that they could read each other's thoughts. They formed an alliance that made them very prone to getting into all kinds of mischief. They were not the equivalent of two high-energy fun loving kids—they were like four.

So as I was starting school, they were leaving sixth grade with a reputation of Dennis the Menace and Pippi Longstockings.

It was decided by my first grade teacher that I would not be like my twin brother and sister. It was decided that I would be disciplined and punished from the very beginning. If I missed a word during reading class then I was shaken and taken to the principal's office. If I did not hear a question then I was sent to the principal's office. After awhile I was told to go to the principal's office at the start of each day whether I did something wrong or not. This is how I missed most of first grade. The principal never questioned me as to why I was there. I think he must have approved of the way I was being molded so I would not be like my brother and sister. I would just sit under a wall hung bookcase and waste my first grade away. I was put on the shelf much like the books. I thought that I must be bad as only bad boys are sent to the principal's office. I did not tell my parents because I was embarrassed and I did not want them to think that I was a bad boy. This teacher hated little boys and withheld her love. It had serious consequences—almost disastrous consequences.

My parents did suspect that there was a problem when I told them how when I was sick and my teacher shook me for missing a word in reading that it sort of cleared my head. My mother observed the class and noticed other little boys were also being abused.

Luckily, for me, we lived in Columbia, Missouri, home of the University of Missouri fighting Tigers. I was transferred to the University of Missouri Laboratory School. This school was world famous for some of its innovative experimental teaching techniques. It was also where University students learned how to teach with yours truly as one of their students.

I could not learn how to read. I was tested and found to have a high IQ, I was three years ahead of my fellow students in math but I just could not learn how to read. I was a model student and never got into trouble. I, for sure, was never sent to the principal's office. What was discovered is that my first grade teacher traumatized me and, as a result, I had a mental block for reading. Withholding love caused real damage.

The school did not know how to cure mental blocks and they just hoped that I would grow out of my problem. By the sixth grade I was still reading at a first grade level. The school was desperate, I was desperate and my parents were desperate. An illiterate has very little hope in our society.

A new teaching program was introduced in the sixth grade. They thought we should all learn Spanish at a young age. Others in the school thought it would be more appropriate for me to learn how to read before I entered seventh grade.

So, I became a Ph.D. project for a graduate student. When the others were learning Spanish, I was in a private office learning how to read. This man gave me all his attention and love. Perhaps the fact that he was a man helped me open myself up to him because he did not look like my last reading teacher.

In one semester I advanced from first grade reading level to sixth grade reading level. Oh, the power of love. He not only taught me to read, he taught me to love reading.

I was on the honor roll in high school, dean's list at the University of Missouri and I currently read about a book a week. I own a personal library of over 5,000 volumes. So I guess you could say that I got over my reading problem but I think I was lucky. Many children fall through the cracks in the system when all they need is some one-on-one help and love. Love is the cure for love denied.

Creating A Life Plan for Love

It is more blessed to give love than to receive love.

SELF LOVE

I sent the club a wire stating, PLEASE ACCEPT MY RESIGNATION. I DON'T WANT TO BELONG TO ANY CLUB THAT WILL ACCEPT ME AS A MEMBER.

**--Groucho Marx (1890 - 1977)
Humorist**

We must have a healthy self-esteem and love ourselves before we can love others. It is crucial that we build that self-esteem without letting our ego eat our brain. Most obnoxious, narcissistic, self-centered people are really people with low self-esteem. They are simply overcompensating for their low self-image. Those who have suffered from little or no love as children typically have low self-esteem and believe that they are unlovable and unworthy. And yet they are so starved for love that they are almost sick from the longing. The tragedy is that when love is given to them, they either discount it, don't believe it is real, or they think that the person is well meaning and mannerly but that person does not really love them. Or they can be like Groucho Marx and lose respect for the other person, as they believe that only idiots would love them. These people will continue to be unloved because they stop it before it can happen. They find reasons not to believe. They wonder why they have no friends. Most of the time the reason is that they did not respond to the outstretched hand because they did not think it was real or they had no respect for it.

What can we do about lack of self-love and low self-esteem? For some people it can take a lifetime to overcome not being loved. A few never get over it. Some never even realize that there is a problem so they never work on a solution. Most do not want to admit that they have low self-esteem because that causes low self-esteem. Most people with low self-esteem do not read books like the one you hold in your hands. However, if you want to improve your self-esteem so that you can improve your capacity to bring love into your life then keep on reading. There is a library of books out there on the subject of self-esteem and this book is not intended to be another self-esteem manual. Do a search on Amazon under "self-esteem" and you will see what I mean.

In the mean time here are some recommendations:

❖ Become an expert at improving self-esteem by reading all the best books on self-esteem.

❖ Write down on a piece of paper five times a day while reading aloud "I love myself. I love myself. I love myself." If you have a problem loving yourself then start off with "I like myself." You will be amazed how this self-talk will start changing everything.

- ❖ At the end of the day, write in your journal all the things you did right. Describe everything in your life that is wonderful. Write about friends, family or coworkers who appreciated you in some way. Write about how you appreciated yourself. For instance, you are writing in a journal to improve your self-esteem. Start building an evidence binder that proves you are lovable and worthy of love.

- ❖ Stay away from people whose object is to bring down your self-esteem and bring up their brain-eating ego. They will only try to convince you that you are unlovable. Sometimes this can mean less contact with some members of your family.

- ❖ Be prepared to love others and then find people who will appreciate you for who you are. Love those people and accept their love. Remember pick those people that you admire and whom you would be proud to call a friend—those you want to love. Don't be a love vampire and pick people who you want to drain of love.

- ❖ As you have more affirming experiences that you are lovable and as you have fewer experiences that you are unworthy, your self-esteem and self-love will increase and your subconscious truly will believe that you deserve love. When you believe that you deserve love, you will have it.

Perfect Spouse

- ❖ Find someone to love—not someone to love you.

- ❖ Find someone who is looking for someone to love—not someone who is looking for someone to love them.

- ❖ Find someone who you would be proud to say is the mother or father of your children.

- ❖ Find someone who loves life, loves family, loves friends, loves the idea of facing the world together and going for the big adventure.

- ❖ Find someone who has a reverence for life.

- ❖ Find someone who shares your beliefs.

Perfect Friends

- ❖ Determine your interests and meet people who share those interests. If you like gourmet cooking—go to a cooking class. If you like books—join a book discussion club. If you like volley-ball—join a team. If you go to church—join a Bible study group. The main thing is to meet people that may relate to a common interest.

- ❖ To have friends you must be a friend. Give love and friendship to all you meet.

- ❖ Cultivate and help coworkers with their careers.
- ❖ Stay in touch by phone, e-mail and letters. Make sure your holiday card list is growing each year.

- ❖ Invite these people to your home—spend time with them.

- ❖ Be there for them.

- ❖ Offer help in anyway that they could use you. *"A friend will help you move. A really good friend will help you move a body."* –Anonymous

- ❖ Make new friends each year because many will move away, decide they would rather watch TV and because, as you age, many will die. Some middle-aged people stop trying to make new friends because they think they have as many as they want and they don't want to invest time and money into new friendships. This is a mistake. Your friends should both get younger and older as you age. Don't be like a lot of people who when they reach the end of their lives most of their friends have died. These people are the saddest, loneliest people in the world.

Volunteer

- ❖ Find an organization that you really believe in--one that you would be proud to serve.

- ❖ Make sure you serve people directly so that you can get that human interaction.

- ❖ When you are low and feel unloved, volunteer and start loving some people. In short order you will feel loved.

In summary, if we want to make a life-plan for love then all we need to do is:

- ❖ Love ourselves so we can love others.

- ❖ Find a partner to love.

Love—The Key to Everything

❖ Create a program to constantly create new friends and new family. Love these people.

❖ Volunteer and give love.

Until one is committed, there is hesitancy, the chance to draw back, always ineffectiveness. Concerning all acts of initiative there is one elementary truth, the ignorance of which kills countless ideas and endless plans: That the moment one definitely commits oneself, then providence moves, too. All sorts of things occur to help one that would never otherwise have occurred. A whole stream of events issues from the decision, raising in one's favor all manner of unforeseen incidents and meetings and material assistance which no man could have dreamed would come his way. Whatever you can do or dream you can, begin it! Boldness has genius, power, and magic in it.

**--Johann Wolfgang von Goethe, 1749-1832
German poet, novelist, playwright, and natural philosopher**

Chapter 4

Health—Make it Better and Better

Of all the self-fulfilling prophecies in our culture, the assumption that aging means decline and poor health is probably the deadliest.
**--Marilyn Ferguson, 1938- author of
The Aquarian Conspiracy**

Be careful about reading health books. You may die of a misprint.
**--Mark Twain, 1835 – 1910
American Humorist**

Why You Should Make a Life-Plan For Health

THERE is no question that when you feel better you do better. It would seem that an Exceptional Life would be easier to achieve if only one had perfect health. But there are many examples of people with life threatening illnesses, injuries and handicaps that achieved greatness in spite of or maybe because of their imperfect health. Franklin D. Roosevelt was confined to a wheel chair and became the 32nd President of the United States and the only president to serve four terms. Helen Keller was blind, deaf and at first unable to speak and she inspired the world with her speeches, books and articles. Lance Armstrong contracted testicular cancer and was not expected to live. Through his attitude toward victory Lance beat cancer and was the first cancer survivor and human being to win the Tour de France seven times. There are many grossly overweight people who have gone on to an Exceptional Life. There are many elderly people in poor health who started late and finished with an Exceptional Life. Whatever health problems you have, many have also had, or had worse, and still lived an Exceptional Life. The world desperately needs you and what you have to offer so much so that we cannot let health be an excuse for giving up.

We must play the cards we have been dealt. Whatever our infirmities, we must make the best life possible. And part of making the best life possible is to make the best health possible. We all know that our health is one of the most important factors for having the energy to produce the Exceptional Life. In fact, although perfect health is not a requirement for the Exceptional Life it certainly makes it more likely. That is what this chapter is all about, improving our health. As Émile Coué said "Every day, and in every way, I am becoming better and better." We need to have this attitude.

SALT

Let me take you on a little journey of the imagination. Can you imagine perfect health? What would our world be like if everyone had perfect health? Imagine that a scientist invented a pill that was made out of a common substance and that this pill would guarantee perfect health with maybe the exception of those who had been involved in an accident. Now imagine that this scientist put the patent in the public domain and it only costs 2 cents a day and those who could not afford it received it free. What would happen to our health care world? Like buggy whips, doctors, pharmaceutical companies and insurance companies would rarely be needed. Today, jockeys use a shortened whip and we would use shortened health care, needing these people only if we had an accident. No longer would we need them for cancer, heart attacks and high blood pressure for these conditions would no longer exist. Their business would dry up. The medical industrial complex would be substantially reduced just like the buggy whip factories. They would lose many billions of dollars.

Now imagine how this magic pill would come to market. Would the medical industry sit back and let this pill destroy their profits? What would they do to keep this pill off the market? Or perhaps they would let it come to market in some countries.

This was a journey of the imagination and I am sorry to say that there is no such magical pill. However, there are major advances, which we must search out and find as some of these advances may not always be advertised to the public.

Do you or any of your family or friends suffer from high blood pressure, adult onset diabetes, heart disease or strokes? The answer is most likely YES because we have an epidemic going on in this country. I know I have an interest as my family and many of my friends have a history of these afflictions. Let me tell you about an inexpensive "magic pill" for these diseases.

Back in the early 90's research was done into the relationship of sodium and potassium in the diet. It was found that the body can't get rid of sodium without the help of potassium. Potassium links with the sodium in salt and then it can be expelled. Too much salt in the diet is really too much sodium in the diet without any help from potassium. People who can't get the sodium out of their system see it build higher and higher. As it builds, it first causes high blood pressure. As it builds further then adult onset diabetes occurs. Then the sodium poisoning causes heart disease and finally strokes. High blood pressure is only the first symptom of sodium poisoning. Scientists discovered that reducing salt intake and taking medications was not the answer. Taking less salt still added to the total sodium in the body and the medication only reduced the symptoms—the sodium was still poisoning the body. The answer was to pair sodium chloride (salt) with potassium chloride and to have a salt that could be handled by the body. That way any sodium that was put into the body would immediately be eliminated by being paired with the potassium. The physiology requires sodium to be paired with potassium if one wants to get rid of the added sodium.

    After studying the science in great detail using double blind studies, Finland's public health department required that its entire population use balanced sodium chloride/potassium chloride salt in all manufactured food products and for the table. They knew their people would not just give up salt so they introduced a salt that was healthy and still tasted like any other salt. This was perhaps the biggest study of all and it was for the entire world to see. It was important because it dealt with the entire country of all its citizens, young, old, men, women, people of all walks of life—the entire population. It must be said that Finland must have been pretty sure of the facts to change the entire nation's food supply in such a manner. It was an incredible public health project. Did it work? Did this new salt improve the population's health? It resulted in a significant decrease in high blood pressure and a 60% decline in deaths from both strokes and heart attacks and this for all of Finland. Now 60% is a HUGH number. It is such a HUGH number that everyone should know about this new balanced salt. I wonder why we have not heard about this in America. I wonder why this salt is not available in grocery stores or health food stores. I wonder why so called "health" food and other foods have high levels of sodium salt in the ingredients with no potassium salt to offset the sodium. This is proven science and there is no reason why we should keep poisoning ourselves with sodium when we know how to fix the problem. The Romans were brought down from lead poisoning because they thought the lead sweetened their wine. We may be brought down, like the Romans, by another kind of poisoning--sodium poisoning because we think the salt improves the taste of our food. But now that you know, you can do something about it.

Health—Make it Better and Better

Thousands die of strokes and heart attacks every year. Billions of dollars in blood pressure medication, diabetes medication, heart disease medication and stroke medication are sold every year. Perhaps Finland might be on to something with a 60% success rate. If we adopted Finland's lead how many lives would we save? How much pain and suffering would be reduced? How much money would the medical industrial complex lose?

This balanced salt is sold in seventeen countries under the brand name, Pansalt but not in the USA. It is, however, sold in this country under another brand name, Cardia Salt and can be found on the Internet. Search for Cadia Salt on Froogle.com.

If you are interested in reading about the scientific studies that are being ignored in our country, then read *The High Blood Pressure Solution-- A Scientifically Proven Program For Preventing Strokes and Heart Disease* by Richard D. Moore, M.D., Ph.D. This is not an unproven health fad. This book was primarily written for physicians. It is very interesting reading with all the scientific information and studies. This health information could save your life and your family's life.

Dr. Moore recommends that this information be used in partnership with your physician. Going off blood pressure medication should always be done with the monitoring and advice of your doctor.

Perfect health is part of perfect success. There is power in information. Find out about health success in the rest of the world. Your life may depend on it.

PAIN

There once was an ancient disease, which made one feel no pain. It was almost like one took a tranquilizer, a double martini, and state of the art painkiller all at once. But this disease was considered one of the most horrifying curses that could befall a family. It was not a respecter of social class. Rich, poor, powerful, weak, all could be afflicted.

Now our culture hates pain. In extreme cases, perhaps physicians would love a pill if it could mimic this disease. But let me give you some additional history about this ancient disease. Because people felt no pain, they would injure themselves. They would stub their toes, catch their fingers in a door and twist a key in a lock too hard until their fingers bled. But they gave little notice because it did not hurt. The injured fingers and toes would be knocked again and re-injured and still there was no pain. Eventually, some would become infected and would have to be amputated—still no pain. These people would become disfigured from all their accidents and all their amputations. Many would lose their eyesight because they would forget to blink. You see they could not feel the sting as the eyes dried out. These people who had a life with no pain were some of the saddest people in the world. Their disease was such a horror to everyone else that they were despised, rejected and spat upon. They were driven from their homes, loved ones and out of the community to live in shacks far from everyone else. These "feelers of no pain" were directed to tear their clothes and shout "unclean, unclean" wherever they went. Although feeling no physical pain, they certainly could feel this emotional pain. They suffered from leprosy.

Pain is a persuasive communication that something is seriously wrong. If we ignore or block it then we risk catastrophic problems because we continue to do the wrong thing that makes us ill.

Many of today's doctors seem more interested in eliminating pain and symptoms than in curing the disease. I believe that pain and symptoms are a way for our body to communicate with us that we are doing something wrong and that we need a cure. As the pain and symptoms increase the message is getting louder that something serious is happening.

Certainly there is a place for painkillers however they can also be abused.

Do not believe that all is being done for you if the doctor is only relieving the pain and symptoms. If he or she is doing nothing about a cure then it is up to you to take on the responsibility for finding your own cure. Don't let the doctor convince you to give up on your cure.

ARTHRITIS

My wife cured herself of crippling arthritis. Joan was a young woman, only in her thirties, when she started feeling like a very sick woman with pain in every joint. It was so bad that I had to help her out of the bathtub because each movement caused pain.

Joan had a career in busy downtown Seattle and she frequently had appointments in several different office buildings. So it was not uncommon for her to walk from one appointment to another. This was a problem. You see her feet ached so badly from walking that she had to walk very slowly. Sometimes she could not make it across the street before the light changed. One time a motorist even yelled out- --HURRY UP GIMP! This was also painful.

The doctor said there really was no cure for arthritis and the only thing they could do was to reduce the swelling in the joints and relieve the pain through medication. She took this medication until one day the pharmacist asked her a question. "When was the last time you had your heart checked?" It was true this medication would relieve the symptoms associated with arthritis. But it was also true that Joan could look forward to an early death from the medication's long-term adverse affects on the heart. This was NOT acceptable! Other arthritis medications are very much in the news today because they also have adverse effects on the patient's heart. Pharmaceutical companies are being questioned and some pills are even being taken off the market. It is suggested that others just put a warning on their package because it is believed that it is better to cause heart damage long-term than to have the patient in misery. In other words: "Here is a pill to relieve your pain and eventually it will permanently remove all pain because you will be dead." Hippocrates, the father of medicine, main precept was: "First, do no harm." Is our medical community forgetting their oath?

Needless to say, this warning from the pharmacist was a wake-up call for us and we decided to take responsibility for our own health instead of handing is over to our physician.

We did do our own research at the library and sought out a naturopathic physician. Let me tell you what we found. Doctors in Europe had made great progress with arthritis. They associated arthritis with the body's response to allergies or toxins. So the trick to beating arthritis was simple---eliminate the allergic substances and all toxins in the body.

Guess what? We all have allergic substances and toxins in our systems. Most of the time our organs can eliminate them through normal processes. However, when our body can't, we get sick, lose energy, stop thinking well and grow prematurely old.

Joan went through a detoxification of her body by fasting and using other cleansing methods. She started drinking filtered water instead of city water. She found out what foods she was allergic to and eliminated those foods from her diet. She had tests for toxins in her system and was found to have high levels of copper. Her body did the entire cure because it was given a chance to "catch up" with eliminating the toxins through the fasting process.

A few years later a company in our neighborhood was fined for dumping copper chemicals into the ground water. Our city water had toxic levels of copper and we were unknowingly being poisoned. Now all we drink is highly filtered water, filtered by reverse osmosis with a gang of five other filters.

Health—Make it Better and Better 57

This was twenty years ago. Joan still has no signs of arthritis. If we had not done our research and taken responsibility for a cure we would have been out many thousands of dollars in doctor bills, medication and higher insurance premiums. The disease would have continued to progress and Joan would have been in pain and agony. But the most horrifying scenario is that I could be writing this chapter without Joan as the medication could have destroyed her heart.

Do we have toxins in our body that may be causing premature aging and disease? Be assured that in the American culture we are almost guaranteed to have these toxins.

As we make our resolutions for better health, fast one day a week drinking only water, fresh made juice or homemade vegetable broth (the kind without sodium salt). It gives the body time to catch up and makes us rejuvenated. It makes us smarter, full of energy and less prone to all diseases. It lets our body keep us healthy instead of using intervention from medical professionals. What is the first thing the body does when it gets the flu? It makes us nauseous so that we will eliminate toxins through vomit, perspiration and diarrhea. Our body cleanses the system so it can cure the system.

Most cultures and religions recognize the value of fasting. It can be found in the Jewish, Christian, Moslem, American Indian, Hindu and Buddhist traditions. Perhaps "resting on the seventh day" really means letting our body rest from processing food so it can have a chance to prevent disease.

If fasting has been a part of mankind's heritage from the beginning of time then why did we in America forget the value of fasting? Because with a culture of prosperity and consumption it is counter intuitive to think that by abstaining temporarily from consumption we can actually have more. This is a case where LESS really is MORE.

Try fasting one day a week. I like fresh squeezed orange and grapefruit juice. I make a terrific vegetable broth that I just love (email Recipe@DuNard.com for the recipe) I also like freshly made carrot and other vegetable juices. One of the healthiest trends that I see happening in many cities is the popularity of juice bars. What a great idea for health but also what a delicious idea.

If you try a fast at least once, I believe you will feel so good that you will want to make it a weekly event.

WALK

Consider walking. When was the last time you enjoyed a long walk through a beautiful landscape? Did you have a friend with you and was your conversation more lively and animated? Did the walk leave you with a joy and satisfaction that made you think: Why don't I go on more walks? Why don't you?

As you may have noted from the chapter on love, I went to an unusual grade school and high school, the University Of Missouri Laboratory School. This school was part of the University and not part of the public school system. Therefore, I did not ride a bus to school. The lab school did not bus their students. Both my parents worked and there was only one car. My father walked to work at the University and my mother drove to her job at the town newspaper. My mother could not drive us as it conflicted with when she had to be at work. All five children walked every day whether it snowed, rained or the thermometer read 105°. And it was not a short walk. Most of the time it took 45-60 minutes two times a day.

Now let me tell you why this was a blessing. Walking everyday created for me a love of walking. I would get fidgety if I could not walk. My body needed to walk and this great health habit became a habit for life. While on these walks to school I could observe the seasons and watch on a daily basis as small things changed. Walking in the snow and heavy rains was sort of fun. This is what raincoats and goulashes are all about.

But perhaps the best thing about walking was that at the start of my day and at the end of my day I had 45 minutes of private meditation and reflection to think about my life, my school, my friends, my beliefs and my creativity for a term paper. And this was not ordinary thinking; this was the kind of thinking that comes from the blood pumping to the brain while walking kind of thinking. The same kind of thinking that the great Greek peripatetic philosophers did to start Western civilization.

Walking was not just limited to walking to and from school. On weekends if we wanted to go to a movie or get a haircut then we walked even though it was 3-4 miles. We thought nothing of it because we enjoyed the walk.

My father was a professional photographer who I believe had exceptional talent, especially when it came to nature photography. One of his greatest pleasures was to take his family on a hike in the country. We would hike all day along a creek and through the woods. He would take pictures and we would play. Many times it was a spiritual experience and at all times it was rejuvenating. I still must hike in the woods from time to time and my favorite vacations are those where nature is involved; Kauai, HI is one of those places.

We were created to walk. We must walk or the body will start to break down. Our heart is not the only organ that pumps fluids through our body, the legs, while walking, also pump other kinds of fluids. Like the cardiovascular system, the lymphatic system is made up of vessels and valves. However, the lymphatic system has no equivalent pump like the heart, it must rely on the muscles of the legs and breathing to force those fluids through the body. Without walking and breathing hard our body can't circulate these fluids and illness and premature aging begins. Perhaps finding the best parking place means finding the one that is further away.

Think about how primitive man constantly walked just to keep enough food on the table. Think about how up until the last 100 years one lived in the city and walked to work, walked to see friends, walked to shop and walked for almost every activity. The necessity to walk is in our genes.

Doctors can't understand why the French who eat great quantities of fatty cheese and goose livers have low incidence of heart disease. They can't understand why the Italians who also eat lots of fatty olive oil and cheese also have low incidence of heart disease. Some have figured it is the red wine that protects them but I believe it is because they have set up their cities so that they must walk everywhere everyday. San Francisco and New York City are two examples of American cities that were built for walking and I would bet that those who do walk every day have a similar low incidence of heart disease as the Europeans.

When you plan your dream house, plan for one where a car is not needed; where work, friends, shopping, and recreation are only a 30-45 minute walk away. By doing this you will also guarantee time to think and time to be healthy.

Perhaps you are not quite ready for the dream house. Walk where you can in the fresh open air and or use a treadmill. As a last resort, a treadmill gets the job done on a daily basis and you get your 45 minutes of walking and 45 minutes of peripatetic thinking. Don't waste the thinking time by reading a book or watching TV. This is your time to find your thoughts and is one of the main reasons for walking. Those thoughts are worth finding. Many people are so amazed at the creative ideas that start coming that they keep a pencil and pad of paper close by so that they can capture and record those incredible thoughts. After the first week you will feel so energized that you will be addicted to walking.

Just as walking is a requirement for keeping our lymphatic system working, beliefs and choices contribute to our health.

Faith-Belief

There is a great power in each and every one of us that confounds many scientists, doctors and sometimes theologians. This power is the power to heal even when everyone says it is impossible. It is our greatest link to health and happiness.

One thing that all the world religions have in common no matter if you are a Buddhist, a Hindu, a Moslem, a Jew or a Christian most likely you believe in the power of prayer. There is a good reason for this. People who sincerely believe that their prayers will be answered are frequently rewarded with positive results. The news about answered prayers seems to travel fast causing those religions to grow and causing more to believe in prayer. No matter which God is prayed to, the belief that the prayer will work seems to make the difference. FASCINATING!

Religion is not the only place where beliefs are crucial to success. The medical industry also knows that patients who believe in the treatment have a greater chance for success. Those doctors who make patients believe that there is no hope and that they will die in three months are simply ignorant and not scientists. For there is a lot of evidence of spontaneous cures based on faith or belief alone.

When a new medication is being tested, it must go through a "double blind" study. All of the patients are told that they are receiving an amazing new drug. Half the patients receive the new drug and the other half receives a sugar pill (placebo). Those people working with the patients don't know which ones are receiving the placebo. The patients don't know which ones are receiving the placebo. Therefore two groups are "blind" to the information, thus double blind. The reason that both groups must not know is so they do not subconsciously treat the placebo group differently.

Those patients who sincerely believe and who are emotionally excited about the outcome can receive the sugar pill thinking it is the real thing and become well. The medical profession calls this the placebo affect. It is the patients' belief or faith in the pill that makes them well. The placebo affect has cured some of our worst diseases. But it is not consistent because faith and belief are not consistent.

Perhaps we should be studying how to make the placebo affect work every time. The medication is inexpensive (sugar pills) and it has no side affects except possible weight gain. Or perhaps we should really study how our beliefs can create our future.

So we see prayers answered and diseases cured because of our faith and beliefs. Perhaps it is important to pay attention to our beliefs.

If you believe you are too old or too young to succeed, you will be right. Yet there are many who have succeeded who are much older or much younger. If you believe you are the wrong color, too fat, too skinny, not educated, too educated, male, female, do not have enough time, or too much time, living in too small a town, living in too big a city, to succeed then you will be right. But there are examples of many many successful people who were the wrong color, too fat, too skinny, etc. who triumphed without excuse. What you are really saying is that you don't believe in your own success and the above excuses are your reasons. You will be right!

Health works the same way. If we can take to heart the following affirmation then, if we are like many others, it will lead to the right state of mind for perfect health.

My body and all its organs were created by the infinite intelligence in my subconscious mind. It knows how to heal me. Its wisdom fashioned all my organs, tissues, muscles, and bones. This infinite healing presence within me is now transforming every atom of my being making me whole and perfect now. I give thanks for the healing I know is taking place now. Wonderful are the works of the creative intelligence within me.

**--Joseph Murphy,
Author --The Power of Your Subconscious Mind**

Beliefs are the seeds that create our futures. Our subconscious is the soil where that future grows. We can choose to plant the seeds that are beautiful, positive and empowering or we can choose to let the weed seeds of doubt, fear and negativity doom us to a life that we were never meant to live. It is your choice.

Most people are unaware that they can choose. They are unaware that it is as simple as making a choice that is really a no-brainer. Choose an amazing full life! Choose love! Choose health! We must exercise our free will for life, love and health or we could be greatly disappointed.

What beliefs are holding us back? These are weeds—destroy them. What beliefs empower us to live a full exceptional life? These are magical flowers of success—fertilize and cultivate them. Start believing that perfect health is possible.

Making Your Health Plan

In one chapter we are not going to cover in depth what you should know to make a comprehensive health plan. But we can start you on your journey. My philosophy has always been to do what has worked for thousands of years in countries everywhere. We are going to talk about secrets that many cultures practice and which are extremely effective. Along with taking responsibility for your health and never allowing any man or woman to determine your fate, we also recommended in the above passages that:

- ❖ We must cleanse our system weekly of toxins. Fasting one day a week on water, fruit juice and vegetable broth.
- ❖ Lower sodium salt intake and substitute this salt with balanced sodium/potassium salt.
- ❖ Walk daily and think daily.
- ❖ Believe and have faith that you have a great power within to stimulate perfect health.

There is a lot of controversy on how to attain exceptional health. Many educated professionals disagree. That is why I am recommending doing what has worked in the past worldwide. There are many more ideas besides those listed below. Hopefully these will get you to thinking. Perhaps the West does not know everything and perhaps we should use the Internet and the Library to do research.

Here are a few ideas—Be sure to find many more on your own:

- ❖ **Eat organic** with no pesticides, no herbicides and no hormones. Cancer seems to be occurring in epidemic numbers. Children are coming into puberty at much earlier ages. Is it the food? Is our growth hormone laced milk safe? Should we risk feeding our children irradiated or bio-engineered food? Who knows the truth? We do know, however that humans have been eating organic food for thousands of years with none of these strange diseases that we are seeing today. Play it safe, eat organic.

- ❖ **Vitamin C** by some is considered the fountain of youth. Sweden is known as having one of the longest lived, healthiest populations in the world. Their secret—wild rose hips. For thousands of years the Swedes have gathered rose hips to supplement their diet. Rose hips are much better than the Vitamin C tablets you buy at the store. The rose hips have natural enzymes that allow your body to assimilate the vitamin. Plant some Rosa Ragosa bushes in your yard to harvest your own rose hips and in the mean time use rose hip Vitamin C capsules.

- ❖ **Use a sauna.** Remember how Finland reduced deaths in their country from heart attacks and strokes by 60% by simply using a healthy salt? These people have also been some of the healthiest long-lived people in the world. Their secret is the sauna. When the body is ill, it is common for it to produce a fever that kills and cures the disease. The Finnish people simply create an artificial fever with their sauna. If any pathogen is in their body then it is killed with the nightly sauna. Like the American Indians with their sweat lodge, the Finnish people consider their sauna a sacred place. Family and friends tend to be closer when they share a sauna. Because it relaxes a person so completely there is no need for two martinis after work. Those wishing to build their own sauna at considerable cost saving should contact Sauna@DuNard.com.

- ❖ **Eat whole grains**--whole-wheat, buckwheat, rye, millet, brown rice, oats, corn and sesame seeds. Consider buying a stone mill so that your flour will be fresh and not rancid and toxic. Grind it when you need it. Whole grains are seeds that have everything in them including a spark of life that will produce a thriving plant. That spark of life and balanced nutrients are passed on to you. Whole grains are the best food on the planet.

- ❖ **Minerals and mineral water** have been used to cure for over two thousand years. Doctors still send people to spas in Europe to get the "water" cure. The idea is that the body loses certain trace elements over time. We need minerals to live. Drinking mineral water is a good idea as long as the sodium salt content is not too high. Also, consider a good multi-mineral supplement. Do your research.

- ❖ **Eat plain organic yogurt.** Ilja Metechnikoff, a famous Russian scientist did a study on why Bulgarians live so long and have excellent health. His discovery was that the food in the colon, for many people, putrefies sending toxins throughout the body. These toxins, if continually sent through the body, eventually will result in autotoxemia or self-poisoning and result in premature aging, disease and death. In Bulgaria, the people eat large quantifies of sour milk products such as yogurt, kefir and acidophilus milk. These products prevent putrefaction within the colon thus preventing these diseases.

- ❖ **Eat pollen-rich honey.** Pollen is the perfect food with all of the micronutrients to quickly grow a honeybee. Honey has been considered almost a magical food down through the ages and was given to newly weds to insure fertility. Honey can be left at room temperature and never go bad. It was the penicillin during Roman times. Soldiers on the field of battle would simply mix honey with wine and apply it to the wound. They knew nothing of germs, however the wine would kill any germs and the honey would keep any new ones from entering the wound. A few years ago, National Geographic magazine had an article on Russians that were living to 120, 130, and even 150. The interesting thing about the long-lived Russians was that they were all beekeepers. Because they were poor, they sold the honey and would eat only that honey that fell to floor of the hive and mixed with bee pollen. Perhaps eating a little bee pollen and honey would be good for us.

❖ **Eat seaweed.** In Japan where health and longevity is much better than the United States, seaweed is eaten daily. Seaweed is filled with vital substances that are not available in other foods. Natural iodine is an essential for the endocrine glands and seaweed is one of the best sources. As you age, are you gaining weight, losing energy, losing your libido, then it is possible that your Thyroid is not getting enough iodine. Make seaweed a part of your diet. It can be found at ethnic grocery stores and in many health food stores.

❖ **Eat garlic.** Long believed to be a cure-all food for thousands of years, now only recently have scientists found that it really is a cure-all or at least a preventative for many diseases. It can be used for such things as lowing blood pressure, fighting cancer, and preventing heart attacks. They have found that it is truly a multiple cure or preventive super food. Why not eat it or take a supplement of garlic daily? Italian food isn't a bad idea either.

❖ **Research Chinese herbs.** Believe it or not, Professor Li Chung Yun lived to the ripe old age of 256 years. Being a famous professor, he was constantly in the public eye for over 200 years. When he turned 100 the Chinese government awarded him an Honor Citation for extraordinary services to his country. This is a mater of record and is in the government archives. He is one of the only long lived individuals that has been documented all through his life. It is pretty well believed that this man truly lived to 256. Even the West believes it as Li Chung Yun gave lectures at the University of Sinkiang to the curious Westerners. He was born in 1677 and died in 1933. It is believed that his longevity was a result of drinking tea daily that was made of Gotu Kola, Ginseng and other herbs. Perhaps Chinese herbs are worth investigating.

❖ **Become an expert on vitamin supplements.** There is a natural Vitamin E that costs four times as much as other Vitamin E capsules. This Vitamin E has things in it that are crucial for making the body assimilate the vitamin. Do your research and come up with a plan for supplements that could bring you to perfect health living way past the age of 100. Research for the best: E, C, A, B-Complex, Minerals and others.

    A daily multi-vitamin is probably not going to make you meet your goals. It is possible to give you a pill that will meet the government's recommended daily requirements for vitamins. However, don't you want exceptional health? The government's recommended daily requirements only gives you the minimum amount of vitamins that will keep you from getting sick.

❖ **Find a doctor who is reticent to write prescriptions.** No mater what medication you take, even if it is aspirin, it can have a poisoning effect on the system with known and unknown side effects. The main thing to remember is that some medications taken over many years can cause other problems. Find a doctor that is not a "drug pusher" and who is informed in all areas of medicine. Make sure he or she is about working on a cure instead thinking his or her work is done when all the symptoms are removed.

- ❖ Make sure you get **enough sleep**, rest and relaxation. Spend the money to buy the best mattresses and pillows you can afford. We spend a large percentage of our lives in bed. What a waste to spend our lives on cheap mattresses. A good night's sleep is the foundation of our health and will make a great difference in our enthusiasm during the day. If we are tired, then we are not enthusiastic. People who are enthusiastic are happier and tend to get promoted. The American people are more sleep deprived than any other nation. This leads to all kinds of health problems. I believe one major reason Americans do not get enough sleep is because of the effects of TV. Programming and commercials are designed to keep us awake and watching. Light flashes, movement, music and dialog all stimulate something in us that blocks the natural urge to turn off the TV and go to bed. As a result, Americans watch too many late night shows without realizing they are tired. They realize it when they get up in the morning and are too lethargic and unhappy to give 120% at work. Read before going to bed instead of watching TV.

To fulfill a dream, to be allowed to sweat over lonely labor, to be given the chance to create, is the meat and potatoes of life. The money is the gravy. As everyone else, I love to dunk my crust in it. But alone, it is not a diet designed to keep body and soul together.

**--Bette Davis, 1908 - 1989
American Actress**

Chapter 5

Wealth & Prosperity—Cultivate it and Give it Away

Money is a terrible master but an excellent servant.
--Phineas Taylor Barnum, 1810 – 1891 American Showman

The highest use of capital is not to make more money, but to make money do more for the betterment of life.
--Henry Ford, 1863 – 1947 American Industrialist

Money is better than poverty, if only for financial reasons.
--Woody Allen, 1935 - U.S. Film Director, Screenwriter, and Actor

Why You Should Make a Life-Plan For Prosperity

WEALTH and prosperity are all around us. All of nature has the characteristic of great excess. The sky has way too many stars. At least it does if you think God should be more careful with his resources. Look at the extravagance of birds and flowers and insects. We see magnificent odd birds of every color and shape that guarantee ornithologists lifetimes of interesting work. Do flowers really need to be so beautiful, numerous and amazing? Isn't there something sinful in so much extravagance? What about diamonds and gems? Why were they made? It seems that God or some creator went way beyond "just good enough" to magnificent, extravagant and outrageous. Just look at the elephant. You couldn't have a more weird and surprising creature. We are fortunate as He or She was totally excessive in gifts and blessings. Perhaps it is only moral to enjoy our gifts and blessings. Perhaps denying these gifts and blessings is the real sin.

    I, for one, believe that the planet Earth is an incredible gift for which we should show our appreciation. One way to show that appreciation is to check it out and travel all over the planet. I see travel as a pilgrimage rather than excess consumption. But we don't have to travel to appreciate our gifts and blessings. We can appreciate everything around us—the tree out our window, the moonrise, an ocean breeze or perhaps just the fact that we are alive. That feeling of appreciation seems to bring on more wealth and prosperity.

    Now we have been talking about nature and all the excessive gifts and blessing we have received. And I would imagine that most of us would agree that life and its gifts are pretty amazing. In addition, I imagine that we don't mind accepting these incredible gifts. Dreams are made of beautiful sunsets, spring days and smiles on people's faces. In fact, we accept these gifts without much thought. What I find strange is the fact that some people don't understand that everything is a gift—including money. Some people will accept a flower but not a good stock.

    This planet is all about wealth and prosperity and we were all meant to be wealthy and prosperous. It is only when our head gets in our way and we believe in poverty that we tend to become people of lack. Let me give you an example.

Belief in Blessings or Curses

    When I managed people's portfolios, I was constantly amazed at how two groups of people could buy the same stock at the same price and have radically different results. One group was my "winner" client group and the other was the "loser" group. One would think that it was the stock that counted but that person would be wrong---it is the personality of the new owner/investor that counts the most.

What I found is that the positive clients who had every expectation and belief that they were going to win, would win. These people seemed to have a sixth sense that would make them winners in the stock market. They would buy, hold and sell at just the right times. Of course they were paying for my advice and in most cases they followed it explicitly.

The other group seemed to be hopeful but would have fears that they would lose money. They were constantly looking for reasons to bolster their fear that the new stock was a dog. Most of the time they were second-guessing the high priced expert advice. Now, remember, both groups received the same recommendation to buy the same stock at the same time and price.

After I recommended the stock to the "loser" group, most would wait to invest until they believed it was a good stock. That meant that it had run up some in price. So they typically bought at a higher price than the winners who bought it when I recommended it at the lower price. The loser group would also sell at the first bad news or downturn in the stock. They did not have the right mental attitude to be winners. Their belief in failure caused them to make failing decisions that caused failure. They were failure magnets. Their mantra was: Buy high--sell low—Buy high—sell low. The winner's belief in success caused them to make advantageous decisions that created huge success. Both groups had the same opportunity with the same stock---the only difference was their belief.

Are we preparing for prosperity or poverty? Only by looking at our beliefs will we know. Do we look for opportunity or do we look for security? After losing money in the stock market when the dot com's crashed, are we still earning less than 1% in a money market? Are we more interested in saving money than we are in making money?

Answer these questions and you will know if you are currently on the side of fear or on the side of prosperity.

Wealth and prosperity are relative things. We can compare ourselves to others and always find those with more money and so feel poor. We can also compare ourselves to the less fortunate and think that we are richer than Midas. But when we start comparing we start getting into trouble, we either come up short or arrogant. We can start feeding those bad emotions like jealousy, greed, selfishness and arrogance. If we don't compare, then we can celebrate success in others because we know that if they can do it then so can we. We are not jealous. We are only interested in learning success lessons from those people who have climbed the mountain. We may also be able to learn success lessons from those we would have considered poor. They may have beautiful lessons to teach about simplifying our lives. By not comparing, we can learn from everybody. We can also have everybody for potential friends—not just those in our economic class.

OK TO BE RICH

Some of us were taught in church that money is bad and you can't go to Heaven if you are rich. I have noticed those churches still need for someone to pay for the preacher's salary, new buildings and new Bibles. And I have noticed that wealthy members are treated with great respect even though it may not be OK to have money. Psychologists would call this a double bind. The message is: Be wealthy so you can receive respect and help out the church but try to be poor so you can easily get into heaven. The way we think about money and how we have resolved this cultural double bind in our own minds can determine if we will be rich or poor.

Do you like rich people? Do you think that poor people are nicer than rich people? Do you think rich people don't get to go to heaven? Would you like to be rich?

Wealth & Prosperity—Cultivate it and Give it Away

Many would like to be rich but they hate rich people. So, in an illogical sense they would like to become what they hate. Is it any wonder that these people have a hard time with finances? Having double bind goals tends to lead to craziness and also leads to poor performance in accomplishing those goals.

Money is like energy, it is neutral, it can give power to doing good deeds like heating a home for a family or it can give power to doing evil like blowing up an embassy. *When we strive for money, we are really striving for the energy to accomplish our goals.* It is our goals we must look at in the light of good or evil, not our bank account. Of course, if we have no goals and we gain money, then shortly we will have neither goals nor money. The lottery winner historically loses his or her money within a few short years, mainly because of the absence of goals.

It is my belief that when we find our financial freedom we find the freedom to become our best selves or our worst.

Having noble goals like sending our children to the best schools, employing a thousand workers, offering a new product that saves lives, or creating endowments for research on AIDS can only be done with money. It is hard for me to understand that money, which can do all these good things, is evil. I think somewhere along the line the message became warped.

The bigger our goals; the bigger is our need for the energy of money to fuel those goals to their destination. Even Mother Teresa and Mahatma Gandhi needed money to do their great good. Both took a vow of poverty but they still made it possible for great amounts of money to come to their goals. Their goals really were magnets to bring forth the money. Your goals can also be magnets.

Wrestle with your mind until you believe that it is OK to be wealthy, prosperous and rich. If the money is for the purpose of magnificent goals that will help many, then how can it not be OK? Unfortunately, if you continue to believe that money is bad then you will continue to be poor. Determine in your mind today to have huge outrageous goals that will help a lot of people. Write down those goals—see the chapter on goals. Then determine that it is OK to be a millionaire in order to accomplish those goals.

Affirm Money or Affirm Our Purpose

If our goal is to make a lot of money without any idea what the money will be used for then we do not have a powerful goal. Just money as a goal does not excite the subconscious. It is what can be done with that money that excites the subconscious. And the more we make pictures and imagine new lives with what can be done with the money the more the subconscious will go to work for us.

With the right goal, money is easy to find. If one has a billion dollar idea it is very likely that millions will come to that person to try to profit on the billion-dollar idea. *We should be trying to make ideas instead of money.*

I know a man that sits down every day and says: "What are the three high value activities I can do to make $25,000 a month?" He then writes down those activities and goes to work to accomplish them. He affirms $25,000, $25,000, $25,000. His main focus is on money and the attainment of money. He has determined that this is the amount that he can earn and therefore he is going to force himself to earn $25,000 a month. For many, this seems to make good sense. Many of America's corporations have a similar strategy. But I must tell you that this man does not seem content, he does not seem to value his employees or customers. He sees them only as tools and cogs for getting him his $25,000. What is sad is that he is not getting wealthy either. To say it another way, he values money but does not value the people who will get him the money. This is a great disconnect!

Now focusing on money is not the problem. After all, we need to pay the mortgage, pay for our children's tuition or plan for retirement. The problem comes when we focus only on money exclusively. He has a good idea thinking about the three high value activities for his money goal. The problem comes when he does not have high value activities for his other goals. He has created a shallow life of money with no life plan for what really counts. He has not thought about balance and synchronicity.

What if this individual had written three high value activities to make $25,000 a month and three high value activities for his life purpose or reason for being? Would he care about customers? Would he care about employees? Would he care about his friends and family? Would he create the synchronicity to make both goals compliment each other and reinforce each other? What is the likelihood that he would be successful in all areas?

There is something magical about writing our daily high value activities each night for the following day. The subconscious mind seems to go to work to give us ideas that sometimes are brilliant. They can even occur in our dreams. Our days are more productive and our lives become fulfilled. However the caution that we must remember is that for high value activities to create the best career and life one must keep them balanced so that they compliment each other and form synergistic synchronicity. A high value activity for money might also be one for your main life purpose. Without a life purpose the money goal can seem trivial. Canadian Terry Fox had his cancer-ridden leg amputated. He had a life purpose that would not be denied. He vowed to run on one leg all the way across the entire length of Canada to raise $1 million for cancer research. Raising money and helping thousands with cancer was synergistic synchronicity. The energy and power of the goal raised the money and also gave Terry the will to run across Canada.

Write three high value activities for your wealth and prosperity and three high value activities for your purpose, your raison d'être and your reason for being. If you do, tomorrow will be incredible.

THE SURPRISE OF SMALL DAILY SAVINGS

Let's assume that it is not about the money and that it is about our life purpose. As I say, the money is easy to come by if one knows their goals, purpose and raison d'être. The hard part can be finding the raison d'être (please refer to chapter on raison d'être). But once we find our purpose we can find the money.

How many millionaires do you know? You know more than you think. I bet you would be surprised at how many of your friends are millionaires. Many of the people who are reading this book are, in fact, millionaires.

I recently met with my friend, Dr. William Danko, the co-author of *The Millionaire Next Door*. His message is one that all of us need to hear. Most millionaires are normal average people who take a conservative approach to wealth formation. That is good news. One does not have to be lucky, a financial genius or have the right relatives to be a millionaire. We can all be millionaires and it is critical that we obtain our financial freedom. Wealth skills are something that can be learned.

When we retire, do we want to live at a poverty lifestyle, our present lifestyle, or do we want to make that a happy time when we can travel, pursue interests and be prepared for all medical costs? It is estimated that the cost of a comfortable, happy retirement is a lot higher than it was for our parents. We need a minimum or $3,000,000 to guarantee this kind of lifestyle. After all, some scientists are saying that in years to come it will not be uncommon for many to live past their hundredth birthday.

Wealth & Prosperity—Cultivate it and Give it Away

$3,000,000 sounds like a big figure. It really is not. The average person with a plan and dedication to that plan can easily surpass this figure.

Let me show you one small discipline that would guarantee $3,000,000 in your pocket at retirement. ROTH IRA's let you save with after tax dollars. When you pull the money out at retirement there is no tax on the interest or profits. That means you can compound your returns with no taxes.

What if you saved $3.50 (cost of a Starbucks latte) a day in a ROTH IRA--what would your retirement look like?

At 10% compounded it grows to $3,000,000 in 56 years. Who would have dreamed that for the cost of a cup of coffee one could be a millionaire three times over?

What made this happen? It was consistent saving, compounding of interest and tax advantages from the ROTH. And that was only putting in $1,277.50 a year. ROTH currently allows much more.

Perhaps you can't wait 56 years. The time can be shortened considerably if one starts with a savings, puts in more than the cost of a cup of coffee per day and earns more than 10%. The important thing is to start and to start NOW. An excellent financial calculator can be found at the following hotlink:
http://www.soundmoney.org/toolbox/calculators/Savings.php.
Play with the numbers and see where you are right now.

It has been said that JOB stands for Just Over Broke. It pays just enough money to pay the bills. The point of this phrase is that we must invest in other ways of building wealth or we are financially doomed. There are more opportunities now than ever before for finding financial security. The Internet is rich with information for entrepreneurs.

The main areas of wealth formation are:

1) Job or profession

2) Real Estate

3) Business

4) Investments in Securities

5) Internet

The best plan for wealth formation brings income in from all these sources. We are no longer just our JOB we are entrepreneurs. How does your life purpose fit into these five different areas?

Living Quickly--Slowly

No matter how much control and planning we have in our lives we still can be thrown off by what seem to be random circumstances. We could be at the height of our game and the next morning we could wake up to severe illness. In the twinkling of an eye everything can change. We may think we are in control and later be surprised by our total lack of control. Our idea of reality can go from vigorous vital life to one of discovering the mysteries of the afterlife. December 26, 2004, we saw that nothing is certain, when an estimated 250,000 people lost their lives to a huge tidal wave or tsunami.

I am sure many of the victims were just like us, they had dreams, plans and people they loved. The big question is did they put off their dreams, their plans or actions that showed their love? If they had known they were going to die, would they have had any regrets?

Life is a paradox. We must plan for the future as if we are going to live to 150 and we must live as if we could die tomorrow. It is best to do both in balance. If we only live life as if we were going to live to 150 then we tend to put things off and procrastinate. This is where most people find themselves.

Equally, the problem with living only as if we are going to die tomorrow is that we may spend all our savings on cruises and high living and find out when it is too late that we needed the money for retirement. Both philosophies by themselves are wrong but combined, they are just right.

I am reminded of the wise advice of the time management expert. He said: "Work quickly—slowly."

We must live our dreams NOW, start our plans NOW and love people NOW. This is working quickly and living as if we could die tomorrow. On the other hand, we must make grand dreams, grand plans that will last 150 years. And while we do that, it does not hurt to figure out how to love many others besides just our own family. This is living quickly—slowly.

Do you have a book in you that needs to be written? Start writing today. Do you want to start a business? Take the first steps today and get a domain name on the Internet. Do you love your family? Show your love with words and more importantly with action. How will all these dreams and plans and love affect your long-term goals? How will you safeguard your health? Do you take vitamins or supplements?

Don't wait, start living today as if you do not have another day and start projects and dreams as if you have enough time to finish.

Taxes

So we live quickly -slowly knowing that we could die and at the same time knowing that we could live to 150. We know that death is probably going to happen sometime. But what do we know is always going to happen every time? Taxes! We need to look at taxes and make plans for taxes.

Read any good books lately? Have you been paid cash in your pocket to read those books? I have a book in mind that would take you about as long to read as a good novel. Many read it in just a few hours. If I promised to pay you

$5,000 to read this book or if you are a business $3,000,000---would you read the book? Now I must warn you that many consider this book boring. Perhaps the money will lessen the boredom.

I was a Vice President at a major Wall Street firm and one of my jobs was to dramatically, legally, lower taxes for large firms and wealthy individuals. We would take advantage of all the tax laws to do everything that was available to lower the tax burden. For instance, we would convert short-term capital gains to long-term capital gains within a few months. This would effectively lower the tax obligation. We also would defer taxes from one tax year to the next, to the next, to the next thus these companies never paid any taxes. Some very large corporations that you know the names of never pay taxes because of this deferral.

Is this fair? Perhaps not, however there is one saving grace. Most of the tax laws that corporations and wealthy individuals use can also be used by you. Are you willing to spend the time to read a boring book, which will pay you thousands or perhaps millions?

You may say that you have a CPA or an accountant and he or she does your taxes. Great, keep those professionals. However, remember your vested interest in lowering your taxes is greater than your CPA's. It is a bigger deal to you if you save $1,000 in taxes than it is to your CPA. For that reason you may want to know some rudimentary tax laws so that you can structure your life, your business and your estate such that you are working for yourself and your family, not for the government.

Years ago I was looking through one of those yearly tax guides that you see just before tax time and looked under the category *Deductions*. I wanted to see all the possible deductions that one could write off so I could see if any applied to me. At that time, you could write off a snow blizzard and its motel costs if you were in the middle of a relocation to a new job? It just so happens that I was caught in a snow blizzard on the way to a new job. If I had not read about this deduction I would have never thought to report it to my CPA and he would not have thought to take the deduction. Your CPA can only report the information he or she receives.

This yearly tax guide, if read and followed, is the book that will pay you thousands or millions. You may find that even though you have a full time job it would be a good idea to keep your job and start a business on the side. You may find that businesses are treated much better, tax wise, than are individuals. You may find a whole new way to become independently wealthy by knowing strategies for reducing taxes.

It is not noble to overpay your taxes. In fact, it could be considered irresponsible to your family to overpay your taxes. Become aware of tax laws and make it your business to reduce your tax liabilities.

CONTRARIANS

One of the most important skills to wealth creation and prosperity formation is adopting the thinking of one who is wealthy or prosperous. Duplicate the thinking and we can duplicate the results. Some critics of social engineering in the past have said: "You can take the people out of the slums but you can't take the slums out of the people?" Were they saying that these people's thoughts caused their poverty? Perhaps, however that may have been an excuse not to help the poor. Here are some ways of thinking that tend to bring about prosperity.

On Wall Street, there is a kind of stock trader that is called a contrarian. Their underlying belief is that the majority is wrong the majority of the time. They believe that the stock market is emotional and that people get caught up in their emotions of greed or fear and trade their stocks on an irrational basis. When everyone was buying the dot-coms and these stocks were shooting to the stars in the late 1990's, these people were selling. Not only were they selling but some were selling short in order to make money when these stocks crashed. When the market finally did crash and people saw their portfolios go down by 90%, these people were closing out their shorts and buying the very same stocks. Being contrarian can be a very effective strategy if it is used along with other strategies. I have seen millions made with this strategy by going against the masses, going against popular thought, going against "group think."

Being a contrarian doesn't just work on Wall Street, it works in our everyday life and in the business world. Vacation in Europe in the spring or fall instead of the summer. You will encounter far fewer tourists, prices will be lower, and the French may have time to show you love. Don't go to a movie and restaurant on Friday night when everyone else is going—go to the movie on a Sunday afternoon and the restaurant during the middle of the week. Again save time and money.

What is everyone else doing in business? If you did the opposite could you benefit? Most people are sending their newsletters via e-mail. Would your newsletter be more noticed and read if it arrived from the post office? Why not schedule a business breakfast instead of lunch? If you do schedule lunch, schedule it at 11:30 AM or 1:00 PM and beat the crowds and save time.

Should your résumé look like every other résumé? Make it stand out. Put your name in 18 pitch letters in the right hand corner. It shows confidence and says this person is different and should receive attention. It also can be read when the recruiter is looking for your résumé.

If you are in sales, call when the gatekeeper (administrative assistant) is not in the office but the workaholic decision maker is right at his or her desk. 7:00 AM, 12:00 noon and 5:30 or 6:00 PM are great times to call. Sometimes holidays are also good times to call the prospect. Martin Luther King Jr. day is an excellent example of a holiday when

Wealth & Prosperity—Cultivate it and Give it Away

the gatekeeper might have had the day off but the boss decided to go to work anyway. Guess who answers the phone. You are not like other sales professionals when you use contrarian strategies and you could win BIG.

Whether it is your stock trading, your personal life, your career, your health, spiritual life, or any other aspect of your life—THINK LIKE A CONTRARIAN. The majority can be wrong.

ONCE WE MAKE IT, IS PRIDE AN ASSET OR A LIABILITY?

Wealth and prosperity can change our thinking and change our character. It does not have to. I have advised multi-millionaires who are some of the nicest people you could ever meet. These people seem to be open to others and open to new ideas. I have also advised slightly wealthy people who are big fish in small ponds (a person in a small community that has a small amount of success but because he or she is in a small community they have inflated ideas of their real success). Unfortunately **SOME** of these people are not nice and are not open to others and their new ideas. There is no other way to put it other than to say that they are arrogant. The nice multi-millionaires seem to be more "lucky" and are constantly finding out about all kinds of new opportunities. The Big Fishes, on the other hand, have stopped their "luck" and are resting on their past instead of the present or future.

Success can breed the seeds to failure if we do not take certain precautions in our attitudes.

Pride and self-esteem can be good things. Pride caused us to get good grades in school, work hard for our families and pursue excellence in our profession. In fact, if you want to create high productivity in your sales force then encourage your sales people to have pride in themselves, their profession, your company, your community, your nation and the world. People give extra and make greater sacrifices when they have pride and consider what they are doing as contributing to something bigger than themselves. The enlightened manager gives compliments in front of other employees and gives correction in private. The enlightened manager searches for gold and what is good in the employee and reinforces the good to create pride and self-esteem.

Every advancement in mankind started with pride and self-esteem. The end of the Dark Ages and the start of the Renaissance would never have happened without pride. But it almost didn't happen. Girolamo Savonarola, the 15th Century religious zealot, railed against pride and vanity. He considered it a sin and organized huge "bonfires of the vanities." These fires burned priceless art, jewelry, and fancy clothing. He created an atmosphere similar to Oliver Cromwell's Puritanical England. It was an atmosphere of fear and shame instead of pride and celebration. Fortunately for us it did not last. Savonarola was burned at the stake at the same place where he had burned the "vanities." Within twenty feet of this place Michelangelo Buonarroti originally placed his famed _David_. This is considered one of the greatest sculptures ever created. Could it have been made without some form of pride?

But when does pride become a bad thing? When does it get out of hand? When does it stop our "luck" and we become like that Big Fish in a small pond?

We know when we have too much pride:

- ❖ When we start thinking we have all the answers. The truth is—we don't.

- ❖ When we stop valuing other people and stop giving them respect and dignity. The truth is—we get what we give and people deserve to be valued.

❖ When we are arrogant. Actually—arrogance is a form of insanity based on illusion. There are many reasons why arrogance or pride comes just before the fall.

So, how do we keep having the good kind of pride with the good kind of self-esteem without going overboard and letting it develop into the bad kind of pride that is sick? We temper our pride with an equal amount of humility. That means high self-esteem without delusions of grandeur. Bill Gates is an amazing guy but he did not create Microsoft. He helped, but so did thousands of employees and more importantly millions of customers. I think he realizes that he can make mistakes. It is when he starts believing he can't because of past performance that he will start the company on a spiral down.

Feed your pride and self-esteem but also feed your humility. Keep them in balance. Do the same for your employees, your children, your spouse, your friends and strangers. This is the single most powerful thing you can do to encourage the advancement of mankind.

Summary

So we have agreed that it is OK to work toward wealth and prosperity. That there is nothing wicked about having money in the bank. That most good done in the world has required money. That, in fact, money is the fertilizer to the roots of all good. And it can equally be the fertilizer to the roots of all evil. We found that goals, dreams, our purpose and our greater good will most likely require money. Money should never be the goal, however it is the life-blood of our goals and gives energy to our goals. If we have noble goals but are too noble to raise the money for those goals then we are sabotaging our own goals and in fact are traitors to our own life purpose.

We have discovered that being a person of poverty and being a person of wealth hinges on the difference in our attitude and the difference in our thinking. If we think with fear, we will be right and life will give us something to fear. If we think with positive expectations then life will prove us right and give us incredible opportunities and wonderful coincidences. We will be lucky.

Making your wealth and prosperity plan

Before we make our wealth and prosperity plan we must have a reason, a motivation, a yearning and a passion for why we need wealth and prosperity. Just having a nice house, a fast car and all the other accoutrements of money is not enough motivation and it is not enough to make us do our best work. Only our best work and our best thinking will give us our best wealth and prosperity.

- ❖ Find your raison d'être and purpose in life (see chapter on this topic). This will give you the motivation and will to create the wealth and prosperity that is needed to finance your raison d'être, reason for being, and life purpose. You are no longer working for money—you are working for your purpose.

- ❖ Do whatever it takes to get your head on straight about money. If your purpose is OK then money to finance your purpose is OK.

- ❖ Emulate the thinking of prosperity consciousness. Expect good and look for opportunities. Be a contrarian and look at the world in a different way. Take the path less traveled by—there are fewer obstacles. March to a different drummer. Reject fear and poverty consciousness.

Wealth & Prosperity—Cultivate it and Give it Away

- Knowing your raison d'être and purpose, create a complimentary plan that will speed you toward success in the following areas:

    Job or profession
    Real estate
    Business
    Investments in Securities
    Internet

    These are areas of wealth and prosperity formation. However, they should be structured so that they relate to your raison d'être. Pick a job or profession that is a stepping-stone to your life purpose. Buy real estate that will appreciate but will also serve your life goals and dreams. Start a business that is a stepping-stone to your reason for being. Invest in securities that will make the world a better place and will finance your raison d'être goals. Become an expert with all the power of the Internet and use it for your raison d'être.

- Study, read, go to seminars and become an expert in your job or profession, real estate, tax laws, business and investments, securities, and the Internet. Become someone who prefers to read rather than watch TV. Become an expert on wealth and prosperity and how it relates to your raison d'être.

- Create a timeline for your purpose in life. Create a corresponding timeline for needed wealth and prosperity that is related to your purpose. Create your synchronized plan.

Debt Destroys Wealth

Our culture is a culture of debt. Students graduate and start adult life with paralyzing student loans. They then buy cars, things, and homes to forever be slaves to the American debt complex. They stay in jobs they hate and then when their children start college, they go into further debt and even more debt when they pay for their weddings. This life of debt only makes the banks wealthy—not you. America has more debt per capita than any other country on Earth. Is it any wonder most people feel trapped and unprepared for retirement? **THIS IS NOT FOR YOU!**

If you have any auto loans, credit card debts or even home loans, then you are hurting your chances for a prosperous life. Although it may seem daunting, you can be debt-free. The best book on this subject is: *The Total Money Makeover* by Dave Ramsey. Buy it today and stop the cancer that is eating your prosperity. Go to http://www.DuNard.com and click on "Recommended Books."

Chapter 6

Balanced Goal Planning—Real Freedom

A study revealed that people who simply wrote down their wants and put the list away, discovered a year later that 80% of what they wrote came to be.
--Brian Tracy, American business success expert

When you know what you want, all you really have to do is think it and feel it. That's it. The universe-the spirit of all that exists--will pick up your signal and project it.
--Andy Griffith, American actor

In absence of clearly defined goals, we become strangely loyal to performing daily acts of trivia.

Unknown

Why You Should Make a Life-Plan of Balanced Goal Planning

THINK about the best vacation you ever had. Did you just one day decide to jump in your car and hit the open road? Or did you do some planning and research? Now I could be wrong, but I would guess that the best vacation you ever had was the one in which you planned in the greatest amount of detail.

I think of the most incredible adventure my wife and I ever took. It was an amazing trip to Italy. Our research started with Rick Steve's book *Europe Through the Back Door*. Our goals included adventure, history, culture, great food and learning to get around without speaking the local language. Rick's book taught us how to meet these goals. We were able to plan in great detail. We knew about every city that we visited. We found what we considered to be the best hotels (small hotels that cater to Italians instead of rich Americans). We got our phrase book and took the plunge with our backpacks, our discounted plane tickets and our courage to enter a foreign culture.

Now, if vacations can be made so much better by figuring out goals, researching alternatives and making plans, then doesn't it seem to reason the same process could be used to make all aspects of our lives much better?

Goals, like any good vacation, must be fun, exciting, and have the power to grab our imagination. The secret to accomplishing these goals is to pick goals that YOU really care about. Let me emphasize "YOU". YOU must care about these goals; therefore, they can't be goals that you adopted because other people told you that you should have them. Your parents want you to be a doctor. Do you want to be a doctor? Your rich friends think you should own a Mercedes, BMW or a Lexus. Do you like these kinds of cars? Your spouse thinks you should color your hair. Is this your style or do you just want to keep your spouse happy? The main point of goals is first *"know thy self."* The goals others choose for us tend to waste our energy, spin our wheels and cause us to go in the wrong direction. Adopted goals tend to sabotage our real goals. It is important to recognize them and eliminate them.

So we know that it is important we pick fun and exciting goals that are ours and ours alone. We know that where our heart is so also will be our actions. Most of us are pretty good at setting goals and plans for vacations but fall short when it comes to other areas of our lives. We can't just be taking vacations all the time like some retired people I know. To be truly happy we must have a balanced life with fun, exciting goals that have passionate outcomes in all areas of our lives. Of course not all of our goals have to be fun. We may choose to work hard at a job we hate because it is a stepping-stone to a goal that is very important to us. This goal must be the motivator for us to walk through fire. This is the real goal, not the hateful job, that moves us to action.

A balanced life of goals, however, still misses the mark. Many people will set up an elaborate process to figure all the goals in all areas of their lives. They are excited at first but soon they lose interest and ignore their goals. Why, after going to all that work, do they give up? They give up because they have not built their goals on the foundation of their raison d'être , their reason for being, and their purpose. They give up because they build it on something their heart thinks is trivial. They give up because they don't know themselves well enough to know what is of paramount importance. They don't even know that they are supposed to find their raison d'être and find that paramount importance.

If you haven't done it yet, then put everything aside today and put all your energy into finding your raison d'être, your purpose in life and your ultimate foundation of paramount importance. It may take several weeks or months before you know for certain. But like the man who wanted strong oaks in his yard and was told by his neighbor that they take too long to grow. His reply was: "Then, I better plant them now. I have no time to lose." Start finding your raison d'être now—you, also, have no time to lose. Your raison d'être is why you are here—ignore it and you ignore the most important thing in your life.

FINDING BALANCE IN OUR GOAL PLANNING

What do you do with your free time when you are not working? During our non-work time we have an opportunity to change our lives and go for our dreams. If we are not fulfilling our destiny through our work then these non-work hours are the only small amount of time we have to make a difference. Many, when they retire, simply do more of what they did during their off hours when they worked. They watch more TV and go on more trips. I am sure this is not what you envision for your destiny? Let's find out what you do envision.

We are multifaceted people. We are not our jobs, our position or title. We are, in fact, people with the power to change the world. That is, if we would only wake up and realize this fact. We are spouses, lovers, parents, artists, thinkers, employees, business people, children and spiritual beings. We are even much more than that; we are potentially everything our ancestors ever were and everything that future man can be. We are infinity ready to happen. We are magical people. It is up to us to open the door to our own power and potential. It is up to us to wake up.

Writing down your goals is one of the first steps to releasing great power.

We hear that we should have a balanced life with balanced life goals. It is true that if we balance all areas of our life then we will tend to have fewer problems confronting us from neglected areas.

For what is a man profited, if he shall gain the whole world, and lose his own soul?
                                                            MATTHEW 16:26

From the above quotation we get the idea that it might be good to concentrate on goals dealing with the world but also concentrate on goals dealing with our soul. We could give other similar illustrations of the problems we cause when we do not have a balanced set of goals. The following illustrates the point.

For what is a man profited, if he shall gain the position of CEO, and lose his family?

Or

For what is a man profited, if he shall gain the position of President, and lose his health?

Or

For what is a man profited, if he shall gain knowledge, and lose wisdom?

To live an exceptional life, we must keep complete balance in all areas of our lives and those areas must be in relationship and complimentary to our raison d'être, our purpose or our calling. There are eight areas with a ninth in the center. That center is the raison d'être. It regulates all our other goals so that everything ultimately matters.

Find out if you already have a balanced life. On the next page you will find a man with all the major areas of balanced goal planning. Place a dot on each line to represent where you are in each area. The center represents (0) and the edge of the circle (10). If you are strong in business, put your dot on (10) close to edge of the circle. Do this for each of the areas and then connect the dots. Unless your connected dots form a perfect circle then you do not have a perfect balanced life.

Balanced Life

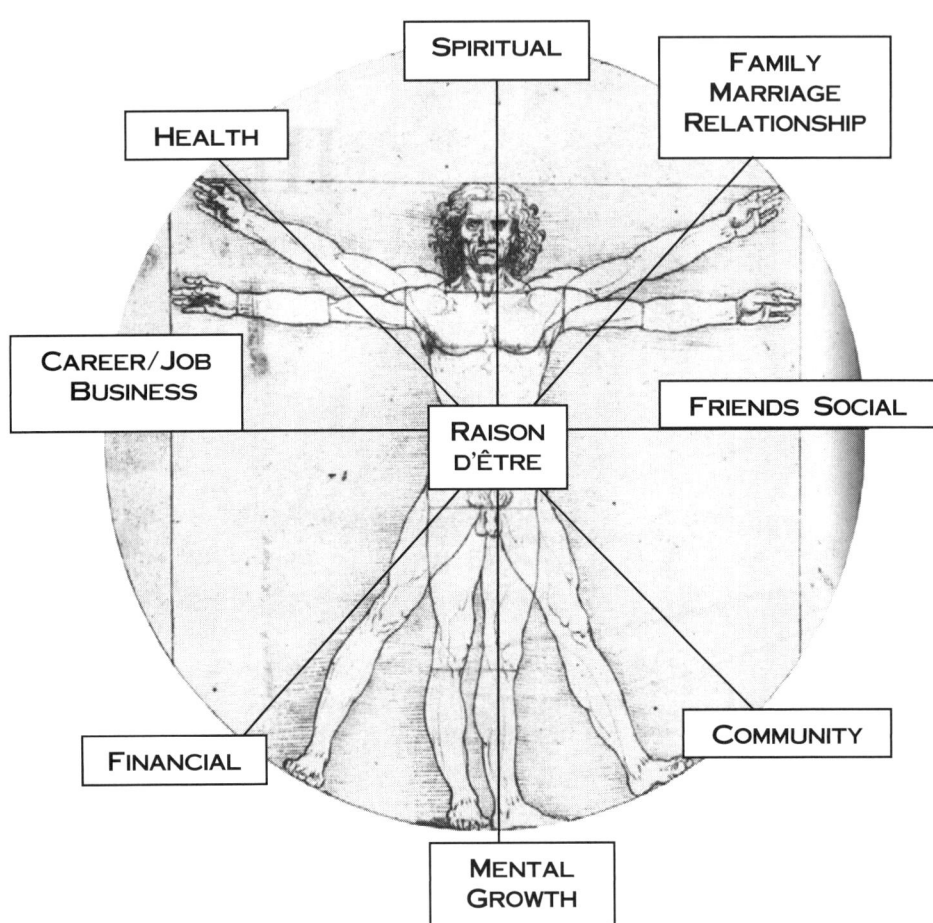

Is your life perfectly balanced? Few are. What would a perfectly balanced life look like?

Let's take the example of Mother Teresa of Calcutta, even though she is no longer with us. Look on the previous page and ask yourself how she would fit in to all the major areas?

It's clear that she knew her **raison d'être**. At first it was to help the poor and dieing of Calcutta, India. Then that raison d'être grew to help the poor and dieing of the world. Most would agree that she was strong **spiritually**. She did not have a traditional family, however she had devoted **relationships** with all she came into contact. Her family numbered in the hundreds or thousands. Obviously she had many **friends** and certainly was not lonely. As far as **community**, that was what she was all about. She devoted herself to her community. **Metal growth** was also strong. She read books and worked on learning new languages. **Financially** she was poor because she personally took a vow of poverty. But her charities that she founded raised millions. All for her raison d'être. We would have to give her a 10 for financial because she did raise money for her missions. Her **job or business** was the same as her raison d'être and she was a real organizer and businesswoman. What a perfect way to integrate the raison d'être into the job. And while she was living, it is said she was a bundle of energy. Her **health** was a tool for her raison d'être so that she could work long hours to get the job done. Without excellent health Mother Teresa would have had a hard time meeting the demands of her purpose in life. Mother Teresa is an excellent example of someone who had a 10 in all areas of her life and at the same time integrated all those areas into her raison d'être. She is also a perfect example of how the universe comes to your aid when you go for your raison d'être.

Happiness or Pleasure

OUR GOAL IN LIFE IS TO BE HAPPY AND TO FULFILL OUR PURPOSE. God wants us to be happy. Our founding fathers thought freedom related directly to happiness and happiness related to freedom. They thought it so important that they put the right to pursue happiness in a prominent part of the Declaration of Independence. But how many of us have made the decision to make an all out effort to make our lives happy or exceptional?

In America there seems to be some confusion between happiness and pleasure. It is certainly pleasurable to be happy but not all pleasures lead to happiness. Just ask the guy eating his third piece of rhubarb pie. Or ask the drug addict, the alcoholic or the spending addict. They gain temporary pleasure and long-term misery. It is no wonder that we have this confusion as from birth we have been constantly bombarded with commercials appealing to our pleasures-- equating pleasure with happiness. When we realize the truth about this difference then we gain a power to choose happiness rather than pleasure.

The idea that I will be happy when I get that $20,000 raise or that new luxury car or that $500,000 house is completely unrelated to happiness. But it is related to pleasure.

Can money bring you happiness? Perhaps, if the money is for buying a long-term happiness goal such as our raison d'être.

I have a friend that told me what it really took to make him want to work harder and smarter so that he could earn more money. He and his wife always highly valued the idea of their children having someone at home that would love them, teach them and do what only a parent could do. House payments, car payments and credit card payments led to the realization that his wife needed to go to work to help make the payments. That meant the children would be raised by strangers at daycare. He told me that the first day of leaving his six-month old daughter off at daycare he just sat in the parking lot and cried. This became his incentive to make money and to move up. The love of his children and wife drove his happiness. It worked, today he is quite successful as an executive with a billion dollar company. Money did help buy happiness but really that was incidental, love bought that happiness.

Our goal in life is to be happy or to fulfill our purpose. Isn't that selfish? I think the above story shows it is just the opposite. If I said our goal in life is to find pleasure then that is selfish, hedonistic, and isolating. There are many lives that have been documented showing that the pursuit of pleasure leads to ill health, unhappiness, pain and suffering. It leads to misery.

Ironically, this is a clue to finding happiness. Eliminate all pleasures that lead to long-term misery, pain and suffering. Add all pleasures that lead to long-term happiness.

Deciding to live a life of intense happiness and fulfillment is like any other decision we make in our lives. When we chose our profession, we made a conscious decision to choose that profession. We then take steps to be qualified and educated. We did not just hope that we would someday be in that profession. We took action! Happiness also requires action. When you get up in the morning ask yourself: "What can I do today to bring about long-term happiness through my raison d'être?"

So when we write out our goals, are we writing happiness goals that fulfill our raison d'être or are we writing out pleasure goals that have nothing to do with our raison d'être? It is important to know the difference.

Values

Rank the following values for your career, with number one being the most important and twenty being the least. For example, if your most important value was health then it would be number one [1] and if your least important value was control then it would be number twenty [20] and everything else falls in between.

Career

- ❖ Admiration [   ]
- ❖ Balance [   ]
- ❖ Competence [   ]
- ❖ Control [   ]
- ❖ Faith [   ]
- ❖ Fame [   ]
- ❖ Family [   ]
- ❖ Freedom [   ]
- ❖ Friendship [   ]
- ❖ Health [   ]
- ❖ Imagination [   ]
- ❖ Kindness [   ]
- ❖ Love [   ]
- ❖ Peace [   ]
- ❖ Power [   ]
- ❖ Purpose [   ]
- ❖ Success [   ]
- ❖ Wealth [   ]
- ❖ Wisdom [   ]
- ❖ Work [   ]

Now, do the same exercise only this time think in terms of your personal life. What are your values when you think of yourself, family and friends?

PERSONAL

- ❖ Admiration [ ]
- ❖ Balance [ ]
- ❖ Competence [ ]
- ❖ Control [ ]
- ❖ Faith [ ]
- ❖ Fame [ ]
- ❖ Family [ ]
- ❖ Freedom [ ]
- ❖ Friendship [ ]
- ❖ Health [ ]
- ❖ Imagination [ ]
- ❖ Kindness [ ]
- ❖ Love [ ]
- ❖ Peace [ ]
- ❖ Power [ ]
- ❖ Purpose [ ]
- ❖ Success [ ]
- ❖ Wealth [ ]
- ❖ Wisdom [ ]
- ❖ Work [ ]

Do you rank your values the same on your career as your personal values? Many people will rank "competence" as number one with their career and rank it close to last with their personal values. This means that they are not congruent with their values. Some say that when the values do not match, then we have lost integrity with ourselves.

Doctor Rachel Naomi Remen states in her bestseller *My Grandfather's Blessings*: *"Perhaps losing integrity with yourself is the greatest stress of all, far more hurtful to us than competition, time pressure, or lack of respect. Our vitality is rooted in our integrity."*

When we live our life by our personal values, we have a chance for happiness and an exceptional life. People who have had life changing experiences like illness, a near death experience or just a mid-life-crisis sometimes wake up and see they were living someone else's values and not their own. They come to the conclusion that life is too short to live with incongruous values. They start doing crazy things by society's standards, however they may be doing just the right thing by their own standards. They become free.

If you wonder which of your values are your real value priorities then look at two things. How do you spend your time and money? Assess your month for time and money spent. Keep track of related values to corresponding spent time and money. Do you spend 45 minutes a day exercising? Then perhaps health is important. Do you put your family on the calendar first before making any other appointments? Then family is important. Do you spend money on books? Then perhaps knowledge and wisdom are important. How do you spend your time and money? Do you put your time and money where your values are? This exercise helps one become truthful with oneself. It also is the first step to effective time and money management. If you do not like where you are spending your time and money then perhaps you are not living by your value priorities.

Values—do you know your true value priorities? They should be closely aligned for all areas of your life. Have you put yourself in different roles with different values? Do you have different values for your job, your family, your church or your club? Find your "real" priorities today and live by congruent values in all areas of your life. If you do, you will have less stress and more happiness—your life will become exceptional!

Now you know, now you can act on your values—your true priorities. As you think about your priorities and values, think about how you can apply these values to measurable goals.

Measure It

When we write our goals it is important to write them in such a way that they can be measured each day. Let me tell you why.

There is a story told of a teenager whose parents got a divorce. One day she comes home and finds her father and mother arguing. As she is standing there watching the argument, her father pulls out a gun and shoots her mother. Then he points the gun at his daughter, waivers, points it at himself and shoots. In a matter of minutes this young girl's world is turned upside down. Her life becomes paralyzed with grief. The way she learned to function again is instructive to us all.

The girl had to learn to crawl out of this hole of sadness. She used a very simple method to create a new foothold, a new handhold. She charted her progress. She found day after day was filled with sadness and grief. But every once in a while, she would have a good day. When she did, she would put a red star on the calendar. These red stars were affirmations that she could get her life back again even if it was for only one day in a month. Pretty soon she noticed that she was starting to have more red star days. This encouraged her further and she had even more red star days. Her life almost became normal; however she would always carry this scar of grief in her heart.

What did we learn from her? Track and measure good things that we want to increase in our lives and they will increase. In her case, she wanted to increase good days so she put a red star on the calendar of each good day. Her mind and subconscious mind were focused on good days. Her mind and subconscious went to work creating good days.

Weight Watchers® uses this measuring technique very effectively. They have the members measure their food points throughout the day and write those numbers on a food diary. The members are focused on their definition of a good day—a specific number of food points or just eating right. At the end of the week the members come to the Weight Watchers® office, get weighed and receive encouragement to continue. These programs work because people are conscious of good eating practices every day and tabulate their results throughout the day and week. They put their mind and subconscious to work creating correct eating days.

Exercise programs also work better if paper is used to tabulate daily results. These results should have a goal in mind. What is your exercise goal?

Tabulating good results and goals does not end with personal improvement. Business also uses measurements to encourage positive results. Salespeople do better if they track their cold-calls, commissions and appointments. Anything we want to improve will be improved if we measure for positive results. But let me stress POSITIVE.

As perverse as it may sound, when we measure for negative results we often times will see an increase in those negative errors. If the young girl had only measured her bad days then it is very possible that she would have become discouraged and given up hope. Bad days would have become her life.

So what are the things we should measure in life? What are the good things we want to improve? That is for you to answer. Some people want better health, friends & family, career, spirituality, finances, community, etc.

For those of you who want an exceptional life, I have developed a generic chart for keeping track and tabulating your own positive results. Over a period of time you will create a better life. Simply e-mail me a request for this chart and I will send it to you completely FREE of charge. E-mail: LifeChart@DuNard.com.

MANIFESTING

What we think about will become our reality. Our raison d'être and goals are a case in point. For some, merely writing down the goals and putting them in a dresser drawer will insure that they will come into reality within a year. By writing them down we have put our subconscious on notice to help us fulfill that dream. Goal writing seems to be a habit for anyone who has accomplished anything that is significant. But let's talk about how this magic works that brings about our dreams in surprising ways. Let's go back and remember how dreams came true when we were children—a time when we had very little money or power.

HEY little girl—HEY little boy, what do you want Santa to bring you this year? Can you remember being asked this question? What was your answer? What was your excitement? Did you get it that year or maybe a year later? What if you could have anything you want—not just in December but all year round? There is a simple process that works every time. We are going to talk about that process.

I remember standing in line to see Santa and wondering what I should say I wanted when I sat on his lap. After all, this was the Man and he could deliver. I had to make something up, as the fact was that I had not ever been asked this question. Quickly, I asked the boys around me what they wanted. All of them said an electric train. That sounded good to me. At that time 95% of all boys wanted electric trains and the Sears catalog had over twenty pages to choose from. I am sure Santa got tired of hearing "electric train," "electric train," "ELECTRIC TRAIN!" I did not get the train that year but I did get it several years later. My Grandparents, as a change of pace, gave each of their grandchildren the normal gifts but also a check for $50 (a huge sum at that time). This was a new development. Guess what I bought. That's right, an electric train.

Now, what we need to ask ourselves is: Did I manifest the train as a "powerless" child? Or did my Grandparents manifest the train with their check? Or, did the Universe manifest the train in response to a little boy's prayer? Perhaps the answer is yes to all three questions.

It is very simple to manifest everything we want. The only reason we don't is we keep changing our minds. Children are born experts at manifesting. Here is the six-step process:

1. **Know what you do <u>NOT</u> want, to do or be and write it down.** As a kid, I knew I did not want another pair of pajamas. Most of us are pretty good at saying what we don't want. In fact, we tend to focus on what we do not want way too much. The pain and suffering caused by what we do not want tends to form scar tissue on our thoughts and we become emotional about these thoughts. Becoming emotional gives power to manifesting what we do not want. Most of us DO NOT WANT THAT! What we focus on the most is what we tend to create in our lives. Because we focus so much on what we do not want, we tend to create a life full of what we do not want unless we take the next step. Most people never get to the second step.

2. **Know WHY you do not want it, to do it, or be it and write it down.** As a kid, I knew I did not want pajamas because they were not fun and you could not play with pajamas—unless you were a little weird. This step allows us to turn negative thoughts into positive. By knowing why we do not want something we find that that something lacks a certain quality. The quality that it lacks is what we want. In my case, as a kid I wanted fun and something with which to play. An electric train would work just

fine. If we hate our job, why do we hate our job? Not enough money, respect, recognition or perhaps the work is boring. It is important to know why we hate our job before we look for another job. Otherwise we will end up with a job, or for that matter, a spouse that is just like the one we left.

3. **Know what you DO want, to do or be and write it down.** As a kid, I discovered I wanted fun and unlimited play. I thought an electric train was a good idea and decided to want an electric train. In a way I had also done step 4 by coming up with my reasons. By knowing what we do not want and the reasons from step 2, we can come up with the opposites and figure out what we do want. So you want a new job and you know why you hate the old one. If the new job does not have all those bad characteristics then what are the good characteristics? Bad job does not pay enough—how much does the good new job pay? Bad job gave no recognition—what kind of recognition are you going to receive in the new good job? Bad job has a mean boss—what is the new good job's boss going to be like? Write down all the characteristics of what you do want.

4. **Know why you want it, to do it, or be it and write it down.** The more reasons you want it, the more emotion and power you put into manifesting. With emotion and power, your goals are almost reality. Your subconscious will now go to work to create or manifest your goals.

5. **Imagine having what you want, doing it, being it and write down a description.** As a kid, I could vividly imagine

playing with the train. I could imagine building a little village and running the train through the Matterhorn that I had created. I was enthused and ready for this train. For the new job we would want to imagine the office in great detail. Imagine the boss and the other workers and how you interact. Imagine customers and fulfilling work. Imagine cashing your check and what that means to your lifestyle. Imagine that lifestyle. Does it include a new house, car or wardrobe? Imagine and visualize until you become so enthusiastic that you cannot imagine your old life. You are creating a new life from the inside out. Your positive thoughts will create that life.

6. **Believe that it will work and give thanks in writing as if you have already received your goal.** I must admit, as a kid, I did not have a perfect faith in Santa. Maybe that is why the train came a few years later. Some call it "Let go and let God." Others just say have faith in the goodness of the Universe. Norman Vincent Peale would have called it the power of positive thinking. We must believe that our goals are fulfilled so that we act and think in a way that is congruent with those goals manifesting. By doing this we open our minds to solutions for their attainment.

What do you want in your life? What makes you excited, enthused and ready to use all your energy, talent, imagination and resources to accomplish?

Protection Paradox—Fear or Confidence

When we write our goals we must make sure that we focus on the positive instead of fear and the negative. It is much better to say: "I am working at the best job that I have ever had. My boss respects me and values me and . . . . etc." Saying: "I am going to quit this lousy dead-end job." will get another bad job.

Are we diligently guarding the front door against errors, mistakes and disasters while we let happiness escape out the back?

By today's standards, I grew up in a large family, a mother, a father, three sisters and a brother. We were sort of unusual in that we all bicycled together. I was the youngest and sat on the back of my father's bike. This was long ago and way before patented children bicycle seats. My dad built my seat out of plywood. The reason I bring this up is so you can see that I was encouraged to learn how to ride a bike.

Can you remember learning to ride? You had to believe that it was possible for a heavy weight to balance on one or two inch wide spinning wheels. You saw people do it but your intuition said that it should not be possible or if it was then it must be hard. So someone you loved encouraged you to try. At first you thought about how you did not want to fall--and you fell. Then you thought how you did not want to drive off the sidewalk or run into things---and you ran into your neighbor's bush. The person helping you said: "Keep your head up, look to where you want to go, keep the handlebars straight, you will find it easy to ride." They focused you on the goal of riding the bike. They gave you confidence. They did not focus your mind on falling, crashing and pain. They focused it on fun and freedom.

It occurs to me that in the business world and our lives there is a place for caution. However, if caution is allowed to rule our companies and our lives then we will lose site of our goals and fall like the child learning to ride a bike. It is easy to become fixated on preventing disasters because disasters are the focus of newspapers, TV and radio. But do we focus enough on our positive goals? Do we focus enough on fun and freedom? Should we keep our eyes on where we are going and keep those handlebars straight? Should we pump those pedals with confidence?

Whatever is true, whatever is honorable, whatever is just, whatever is pure, whatever is pleasing, whatever is commendable . . . think about these things.
Philippians 4:8

Whatever is your raison d'être and your positive goals—focus on these things.

1+1 = 11

Any goal worth two seconds of thought is a goal that involves other people. The best goals require many people working together on a shared dream. Where two or more are gathered in pursuit of common goals--magical results will soon follow.

This last year I spent the day with my friend Mark Victor Hansen, the co-author of the best selling series *Chicken Soup for the Soul*. Now, best selling series, is an understatement. It has sold more than 80 million copies world wide in less than 10 years. Can you think of another author that has sold this many books in the last 10 years? He, along with his co-author Jack Canfield, created an information empire. You can too.

Each story in the *Chicken Soup for the Soul* series connects instantly with the reader's soul. You could say that his products are filling a need that we all have at our soul level.

Did you know that many couples read a story to each other just before going to sleep? It has been found that these books actually strengthen many relationships. If you share a story that instantly touches the soul with someone, you will be closer to that person.

My wife, Joan, and I have been reading stories to each other at bedtime for many years. We have a huge library of short stories, essays, and you guessed it *Chicken Soup for the Soul* books. By the way, we have been happily married for 33 years.

How was Mark able to produce so many products with so much consistent success? Would you like to have similar success in your field? Here is one BIG secret.

Mark loves to talk about 1+1=11. That means if you want exponential success, you must join with others and it will be easy. You, along with one other, will be the equivalent of eleven working on their own. In Mark's case, he was able to join with Jack Canfield and hundreds of writers, advisors, and mentors in common cause for a higher ideal. Is it any wonder that these books and ideas have had such an impact on the world? By the way, 132 publishers rejected the first *Chicken Soup* book. How many of us would have given up after the third rejection?

Are you a rugged individualist that does not need anyone to be successful? Is it working? Do you have enough money to do the work you were born to do? Do you have balance, health, family, career, friends, fun, community, purpose and love? No? (Most of us don't.) Perhaps it is time to join with others to radically increase our power to effect world change.

Do you have a product or service that instantly connects with the soul? Do you need to form a dream team or find others to help you have synergistic exponential power? Let people know about your dreams.

During World War II people were told: "Loose lips sink ships." and "Don't tell your plans or you will dissipate your forces." This made sense when you were fighting an enemy, but it does not make sense when you are living in a world of friends. Tell your plans and you will fire people's imaginations and they will come to your aid to share your dream to build a much better world. It worked for Mother Teresa—it can work for you.

MAKING YOUR BALANCED GOAL PLANNING LIFE PLAN

Imagine that you won a trip to a far off exotic isle. Now this is a place that poets have written descriptions that equate it to true paradise. The water is a clear blue, the breeze is gentle and relaxing, the sands are powdery white and the palm trees sway like they do not have a care in the world. At this moment you also have few cares in the world for you are vacationing on a magical isle. You are alone and strolling along a beautiful beach. Your heart is glad and you know that life has great possibilities. You know that you are at a turning point and now you are getting ready to fulfill your greatest potentials. As you walk, you hear the sound of the surf and feel the cool water as it laps upon your bare feet. You notice that far down the beach the surf has brought a golden object to the edge of the water. You hurry to the object because it looks old and valuable. Remember, this is a magical isle. You pick up the object and it appears to be a thousand year old Arabian lamp. Could it be? Have you found the magic lamp of the Genie? You rub the lamp and a ten-foot Genie appears. You now know that this is going to be a special vacation, indeed. The Genie says: "I will give you ten improvements for each of the eight areas of your life, and not only that, I will tell you what your purpose is in life. I will reveal to you your raison d'être. I will help you have an exceptional life." You stand there shocked. Is this a dream or is it real? Is it a good Genie or an evil Genie? Does the Genie tell you the truth or does he mislead you to a life that is not the life you were meant to live? We will see.

❖ **Find your raison d'être.** Did you do the exercises in the chapter on raison d'être? If not, go back to that chapter, reread it and do the exercises in earnest.

- ❖ **Do the exercises that are listed above if you have not already done them.**

- ❖ **Write down the ten improvements the Genie should have written for each of the eight areas of your life.** Remember to put at the top of each page your raison d'être so that you will connect those goals with your main purpose in life. On the following pages you will find each of the eight areas of your life. Fill out the pages. When you do, your subconscious will have been put on notice. You are well on your way to an exceptional life.

Balanced Life
Spiritual

My exceptional life consists of the following:

My raison d'être is:
_____
_____

If I knew I could not fail; if I knew I had all the time, money, intelligence and special help from the Universe, what would be my ten spiritual goals?

1. _____
2. _____
3. _____
4. _____
5. _____
6. _____
7. _____
8. _____
9. _____
10. _____

Balanced Life
Family, Marriage, Relationship

My exceptional life consists of the following:

MY RAISON D'ÊTRE IS:
_____
_____

If I knew I could not fail; if I knew I had all the time, money, intelligence and special help from the Universe, what would be my ten family, marriage or relationship goals?

1. _____
2. _____
3. _____
4. _____
5. _____
6. _____
7. _____
8. _____
9. _____
10. _____

Balanced Life
Friends, Social

My exceptional life consists of the following:

MY RAISON D'ÊTRE IS:
_____
_____

If I knew I could not fail; if I knew I had all the time, money, intelligence and special help from the Universe, what would be my ten friends and social goals?

1. _____
2. _____
3. _____
4. _____
5. _____
6. _____
7. _____
8. _____
9. _____
10. _____

Balanced Life
Community

My exceptional life consists of the following:

MY RAISON D'ÊTRE IS:

_____
_____

If I knew I could not fail; if I knew I had all the time, money, intelligence and special help from the Universe, what would be my ten community goals?

1. _____
2. _____
3. _____
4. _____
5. _____
6. _____
7. _____
8. _____
9. _____
10. _____

Balanced Life
Mental Growth

My exceptional life consists of the following:

MY RAISON D'ÊTRE IS:
_____
_____

If I knew I could not fail; if I knew I had all the time, money, intelligence and special help from the Universe, what would be my ten mental growth goals?

1. _____
2. _____
3. _____
4. _____
5. _____
6. _____
7. _____
8. _____
9. _____
10. _____

Balanced Life
Financial

My exceptional life consists of the following:

MY RAISON D'ÊTRE IS:
_____
_____

If I knew I could not fail; if I knew I had all the time, money, intelligence and special help from the Universe, what would be my ten financial goals?

1. _____
2. _____
3. _____
4. _____
5. _____
6. _____
7. _____
8. _____
9. _____
10. _____

Balanced Life
Career/Job or Business

My exceptional life consists of the following:

MY RAISON D'ÊTRE IS:

_____
_____

If I knew I could not fail; if I knew I had all the time, money, intelligence and special help from the Universe, what would be my ten career/job or business goals?

1. _____
2. _____
3. _____
4. _____
5. _____
6. _____
7. _____
8. _____
9. _____
10. _____

Balanced Life
Health

My exceptional life consists of the following:

MY RAISON D'ÊTRE IS:
_____
_____

If I knew I could not fail; if I knew I had all the time, money, intelligence and special help from the Universe, what would be my ten health goals?

1. _____
2. _____
3. _____
4. _____
5. _____
6. _____
7. _____
8. _____
9. _____
10. _____

After you have completed the preceding eight pages, go back to each page and circle three of the most important, most exciting and most life changing goals from each page. These are the goals you are meant to work on first. As you complete each of these goals celebrate and write next to the goal "My Life is Exceptional." Please note that the goals, which you have not been working on, can somehow mysteriously get completed on their own. This is because your subconscious has been working on them and they just happen. Re-read them in a year and those that have been mysteriously completed mark "My Life is Exceptional."

See—you are your own magic genie—congratulations!

Chapter 7

Believers, Agnostics and Atheists—In Search of Truth

If you would be a real seeker after truth, it is necessary that at least once in your life you doubt, as far as possible, all things.
**--Rene Descartes, 1596 – 1650
French philosopher and mathematician**

In the attitude of silence the soul finds the path in a clearer light, and what is elusive and deceptive resolves itself into crystal clearness. Our life is a long and arduous quest after Truth.
--Mohandas Karamchand Gandhi, 1869–1948 Charismatic leader who led India to independence from British colonial rule.

The first duty of a man is the seeking after and the investigation of truth.
**--Cicero, 106 BC - 43 BC
Orator and statesman of Ancient Rome**

Why You Should Make a Life-Plan to Find Your Truth

HY are we here? Did we have a consciousness before we were born? Will we have a consciousness after we die? Was there a unifying intelligence or God that created the universe, or

did it just happen by accident out of nothingness? Are we part of the phenomena of creation? Is the creation process still continuing and we are a big influence? Are we partners with God in the creation? If so, can we dialog with God or the Infinite Intelligence to affect our reality? Does prayer work, or are we just insignificant specks of nothingness that exist for a brief period of time and we have no meaning what so ever? Are we nothing? These are the questions that man has been trying to answer from the dawn of history.

When it comes to the subjects of God, prayer, and the soul, we can only take one of three positions. We can believe in God, the power of prayer, and life after death or we can fall into one of the other two groups. We can say we don't believe in God, the efficacy of prayers, or life after death, and then we would be called atheists. The other group has no opinion. This group thinks that it does not have enough information and therefore really does not know if God exists. These people are called agnostics. It is important to admit to ourselves, in our heart of hearts, exactly which group is our current belief home.

> *This above all: to thine own self be true.*
> **--William Shakespeare, 1564-1616**
> **English playwright**

Do not let your culture shame you for your beliefs. Our true concept of spiritual reality or the lack there of is true to the best of our understanding and our understanding should evolve through the years. The main thing is to open ourselves to new information so that we can have a chance to find the real truth to the best of our abilities. This is a lifelong process. However, it stops when we become dogmatic and think we have all the answers. When this happens, we stop growing and start dying spiritually.

If we were brought up as believers in a certain religion and never questioned those beliefs then what does that say about our faith? Is it strong or can it easily be changed like a suit of clothes? If we married someone that was an atheist and we abandoned our beliefs for the sake of the marriage, then did we have any beliefs in the first place? Are we making our religion as unimportant and as changeable as a pair of shoes? Taking religion or spirituality for granted because we heard too many preachers while growing up can make us feel that there is no need to explore or think about the big questions. That is where we would be wrong. As Descartes says we must question everything or, in his words, "doubt, as far as possible, all things." Just because we were raised with a religion it does not let us off the hook for finding out our truths. These truths were given to us by our parents but they are not really ours until we challenge them and accept them in our hearts. We must think, question and research.

If we decided that we are atheists but have closed the subject on new information, then we have also closed our minds. It seems that many atheists come from the scientific community. Now I have always had great respect for scientists because their mantra is "look at the facts—look at the facts." They also believe that there are certain natural laws that govern the universe. But it would seem to me, they have not tried to find evidence for the existence or nonexistence of God. How can a scientist state that there is no God if that statement is based on conjecture and not facts? If the scientist does not have the facts, then it would seem to me that he or she should believe like the agnostic or someone who does not know. A scientist who is an atheist without the facts appears to me to be a hypocrite to scientific principles. The point we must remember is if we believe we are atheists, then we should continue our search. This search takes a lifetime.

Thinking about the big questions can be frustrating. We may not get immediate answers. Books that we read may be inconclusive and contradictory. Retreats, prayer and meditation may give few results. But still we must persist as we are meant to find the light and the truth. If we decided that it is just all too much, that we can't figure it out, we may be tempted to give up and say we don't know and we don't care. If this is our belief then we would be called agnostics. Like the atheist and the believer, we should continue our search to find new information. Giving up is not an option. In everyone's heart burns a desire to know the truth regarding the big questions. Hiding from this desire will not make it go away.

Part of the mystery of existence is that we see though a darkened glass. We see images of flashing enlightenment but mostly we see shadows. Only a few individuals seem to have crossed a barrier to stare in the light of truth. Mankind seems to think these people are fools, crazies and fakes. History shows that they were tortured, put to death and then a few hundred years later they became saints and some, even became a basis for a new religion.. Let's talk about that darkened glass and those shadows.

Plato

Approximately 2,350 years ago the great Greek philosopher, Plato, told an enlightening allegory. This story is incredibly instructive to our times.

Plato tells of a cave where prisoners have been chained all their lives so they can only face the wall. Behind the prisoners burns a fire, which throws light and shadows on the wall in front of them. Other people, who are hidden behind another wall, project shadows of paper horses, birds, and other objects.

Because these prisoners only know the wall in front of them, the images of shadow and light are their whole reality. They have contests to name the shadows. The status of each prisoner is given based on how well they can read the shadows.

But these shadows are not reality. They are only images projected on a cave wall.

One day a prisoner escapes. As he faces the light, his eyes hurt. With great difficulty, he passes the fire and makes his way to the sunlight. He goes through more pain and his eyes are dazzled. But then he sees actual reality. He sees real horses, birds and everything we take for granted. He sees the sun, the stars, the moon and people.

Unfortunately, this man must go back to the cave and be chained with the other prisoners. When he gets there he is no longer good at naming shadows. His fellow prisoners think he is an imbecile. He is no better than a child at naming shadows. They decide that it is bad to go toward the light and out of the cave—it tends to addle one's brain.

Of course, all of his stories about true reality are not believed. For one thing, how can one explain color to someone who has always lived in shadows? So those who had never seen the light considered the man who knew the truth a liar.

These prisoners only saw flashing lights and shadows. They could only receive lies and tell lies for they had no knowledge of the truth.

For me, when Plato tells about the people watching flashing lights and shadows, it strangely reminds me of TV. Could it be that we are also prisoners in a cave watching shadows and competing with one another to name those shadows? Is our life wrapped up in TV, video games, movies, and the Internet? Have we forgotten to leave the cave and go toward the light? On a larger scale, is our existence on this Earth like living in a cave of shadows? We only know of Earth. We know very little of the rest of the universe, afterlife or all of the aspects of its creation. We are like the people in the cave trying to interpret light and shadows.

As in Plato's allegory, coming out of the shadows and going toward the light will be painful for all of us. It is tempting to go back to what we know and back to the shadows where we will feel no pain. Also, we don't want our friends to see us as imbeciles because we have experienced true reality.

We don't want them to hear us talk crazy because we know things that they could not even imagine. However, once Truth and Light are experienced, we don't care. We are in a higher reality—we can see the birds and the horses, stars and moon. The shadows are no longer very appealing.

Leave the cave, go through the pain and find your light. That is why you are here.

THINK

How does one leave the cave? How do we open ourselves to the painful light?

Itzhak Perlman, the great virtuoso violinist, tells a story about his early teachers. While in Israel, he had a teacher that was old-fashioned and one might say authoritarian. She would tell him what to do and he would obey! If he did not, she would "chop off his head."

Then he came to the United States to study with Dorothy DeLay. She was not authoritarian and, in fact, was quite the opposite. She would listen to Itzhak play something and then she would say, "Sugar Plum, what did you think of that?" Being used to the other teacher, Itzhak was taken aback. He would say, "What do you mean, what did I think of it? I'm here to follow your orders." Miss DeLay made Itzhak THINK! She did not think for him. He needed to find his own beliefs in regards to his music. It was no longer according to the music books or the current gospel.

By making him think she helped him to open the doors to greatness. Before he played in "lockstep" with the mechanical perfection of a machine following strict orders. But there was no passion, no soul, no room for the divine, and no room for Itzhak. Just asking himself the question, "What did you think of that?" gave immediate answers for improvement. At least it did for Itzhak Perlman.

When we do our life work are we simply following orders? Do we perform our task in a "lockstep" with mechanical perfection? Do we do our jobs without thinking? Do we do our jobs without passion, soul, room for the divine or room for ourselves? Are we robots? How about what we believe—our truth? Are we following what others have told us to believe or are we leaving room for the divine and ourselves? Are we asking ourselves—What do I think?

My suggestion is to take a cue from Itzhak Perlman and THINK! Think about all aspects of your life. Think about everything and every situation. Don't let others do your thinking. Come to your own conclusions. Find the light!

We have all seen teenagers who work in fast food restaurants act as if they are robots with their brains turned off. Engage them in conversation to wake them up. Advise your teenager to look each customer in the eyes and communicate with that customer. Then advise them to ask themselves, "What did I think of that encounter?"

Once we start asking ourselves questions and start thinking then we are inspired to ask other questions, which will lead us to greatness. Does our work promote genuine, true, wholesome products and services? Do we labor in a job where wisdom is practiced to sustain the planet in love and prosperity? Are we planning for the next thousand years or only the next quarter?

So, in the words of Miss DeLay—"Sugar Plum," what do you think of your life? What do you think of your truth? Are you finding the light?

Perhaps to find our light we need to find ourselves and perhaps our real selves are much better than we think. Miss DeLay only expected greatness from Itzhak.

HIGHER REFLECTION

Who are we—really? Are we children of God or are we nothing? Look at all those people around us—Who are they? Are they the best of humanity or are they the worst?

Part of our journey in finding the light is determined by who we think we are and who others are.

Are we our brother's keeper when it comes to self-esteem? Should we assume that our employees, children and spouse are of the highest caliber?

The answer is an emphatic yes! Expectations drive future actions. No matter what the evidence says to the contrary, if we treat our employees as winners, as hardworking people and as honest people they will tend to meet our expectations. No matter what the evidence says to the contrary, if we treat our children with love, as good citizens, as intelligent people and possibility thinkers then they will tend to fulfill those expectations. If we treat our spouse as the most beautiful/handsome, loving, intelligent and interesting person in the world then they will tend to fill that expectation---no matter what the evidence is to the contrary. Our self-esteem comes partially from the reflections of others toward us. Give a higher reflection and the person will endeavor to improve to match that reflection. But it is not just for others. We should also realize that we are, in our own individual way, unique, valued and someone the world desperately needs (even if the world does not know it yet). We should follow the "impossible dream" to find our truth.

Robert Schuller relates the following story in his book *Self Esteem*.

*In the stage play, The Man of La Mancha, the grand idealist, Don Quixote, meets a harlot named Aldonza.

"You will be my Lady," he announced to this whore. Then he added, "Yes, you are my lady, and I give you a new name--Dulcinea." She laughs scornfully.

Undaunted, he keeps affirming her and declaring her to be what he wants to believe she is. And, of course, the affirmation becomes a self-fulfilling prophecy.

The play continues and the stage is empty. It is night. Offstage a woman screams. It is Aldonza. She is being raped in the hay. She appears onstage, hysterical, blouse torn, hair disheveled, dirt on her face, terror in her eyes, breasts heaving with the fast breathing of a panic-stricken soul. Loud and clear comes the voice of the Man of La Mancha, "My lady!" She can't handle this and screams, "Don't call me your lady; I was born in a ditch by a mother who left me there naked and cold and too hungry to cry. I never blamed her. I'm sure she left hoping that I'd have the good sense to die."

Aldonza is weeping now, head downcast, humiliated, shame-wracked. Then her shame turns into violence, and as her head rises, she screams, "Oh, don't call me a lady. I'm only a kitchen slut reeking with sweat. A strumpet, men use and forget. Don't call me a lady; I'm only Aldonza. I am nothing at all!" She then whirls and runs into the night, but Don Quixote calls after her with a loud voice, "But you are my Lady Dulcinea!"

The curtain drops, but shortly it rises again to the death scene of this glorious dreamer of the impossible dream. He is dying now of a broken heart---scorned, laughed at, despised, and rejected of men. Suddenly, to his side comes what appears to be a Spanish queen in a mantilla and lace. She kneels and prays. He opens his eyes and asks, "Who are you?" "Don't you remember?" The lady rises and stands tall. She is beautiful, perfectly proud and perfectly humble *at the same time. She speaks softly, "Don't you remember?" You called me your lady. You gave me a new name. My name is Dulcinea!"*

Part of our search is to determine who we are. Are we worthy of the light, of truth and wisdom? Everyone is worthy. It is only when we falsely believe that we are not worthy that we block ourselves from receiving these gifts.

Doing What We Can

I am only one; but still I am one. I cannot do everything, but still I can do something. I will not refuse to do the something I can do.
**--Helen Keller, 1880-1968
Blind-Deaf American author, activist, and lecturer.**

Hopefully, we've found a place to be our own unique selves, where the highest of expectations are made of us, and now we can contribute.

The big question is: How powerful are we, really? The answer is that we will never know unless we try.

How much of life do we lose every time we refuse a new exotic food for fear that it would disagree with our taste? Do we lose life when we will <u>not</u> go to new places for vacation? Are we really living when our life becomes a predictable routine with no new growth?

What is more important, however, besides new experiences, is going for our dreams no matter how badly we may fail. Part of those dreams should be to try to find the answers to the big questions. At least we should do what we can to find our answers.

When I was in High School I sang in the Chorus. I loved singing and in fact wanted to become a professional singer. High School was the last time I sang in a group. In

2001 I moved to Nashville, got involved in a church and joined the choir. Now recognize, at this point, I had not sung in thirty years. I may not be a professional singer yet, but my soul is happy, I have made many new friends and my life is enriched. Plus, when my choir gets too much hubris about their abilities, I am able to correct that situation.

But what about those people who were only one and who really changed the world? What about Mother Teresa being penniless in India and wanting to help the poor? Did Bill Gates really think his little startup could change how we work at home and at the office? Did Doctor Professor Longhair know that he would have such a big influence on Elvis and Elvis would have such a big influence on Rock & Roll?

Each of us is only one; but we are still one. We cannot do everything, but still we can do something. Let us not refuse to do the something we can do. Let us do what we can toward our dreams. Let us do what we can to find the answers to the big questions.

We're making our effort—contributing our power of one. Are we doing so logically or emotionally?

SHOULD WE REPLACE EMOTION WITH LOGIC?

How should we think on our quest for truth and beliefs? Is it best to be the logical scientist or the emotional artist? Could we perhaps be both and thereby open the doors to the light?

I recently had a very interesting discussion with a physics professor. You could say he is a high priest of the scientific community. We were talking about the rise of radical fundamentalist like Al Qaeda, those religious groups who are ready to be violent to achieve their goals. Why are they so violent and ready to kill or die?

Dr. Susannah Heschel, The Reverend Jim Wallis, and Imam Feisal Abdul Rauf, Jewish, Christian, and Muslim leaders respectively, discussed this very question. To simplify their remarks, their conclusion was that these groups were working from the emotion of fear. This fear stemmed from a fear of losing their way of life. They felt that the Western world was imposing their values or forcing them to accept their values.

My friend, the physics professor, commented that if we got away from emotions and became totally logical, we would remove fear from the equation and so would not have these kinds of problems. He stated that primitive man and animals worked totally from emotion and advanced modern man should work from logic.

I believe logic can play a supportive role in tempering the ill effects of strong primitive negative emotions. Logic can help the child be less fearful of the mythical monster under the bed. Logic can help the philandering spouse know that the fling is not worth indulging the emotion of procreation. Logic can help the person on the diet remember that they are not starving and do not need to eat more. But these primitive emotions are needed for survival. Logic should come into play when they are over stimulated.

But what if we went overboard and joined the religion of the logical scientists? What if we became Dr. Spock from the Starship Enterprise? Patients would have doctors, who are cold, matter of fact, and seemingly uncaring. This is not a very good bedside manner and I would think it hurts in the healing process.

It is my contention that the most advanced humans are very advanced emotionally and use those higher emotions every day. Passionate emotions are really what move the world. Would you rather have a logical employee or a passionately motivated one? Would you rather have a logical customer or one that is passionate about your products or services?

Passionate emotional music is what lasts the test of time. Handel, Beethoven, Bach are masters of the higher emotions and icons of our culture. The highest prices are paid for paintings that emote passion and emotion. Which would be your preference a Rembrandt, a Claude Monet, a George Caleb Bingham or a logical efficiently painted white canvas with no emotion? Urban Renewal of the sixties caused scientifically efficient housing to be built in the inner cities. Much of this housing was so cold and lacking of soul that it had to be torn down. The greatest advances in our civilization have been inspired through emotion, even the scientific advances.

Contrary to my friend, I believe the higher emotions are what make us human and unique. I believe, that logic is a tool, but higher emotion is where we find the reason for using that tool.

Of course my physics professor friend singled out one emotion, fear, to discredit all emotions. Fear is a negative emotion. One could say that fear is the root of all evil. Most wars are started through fear. Equally, negative logic can cause trouble. Medical decisions that are decided without love tend to cause suffering. Logical decisions that are decided for all the citizens tend to be wrong for most individuals.

So what is the best way to go toward the light? What is the best style of thinking—emotional or logical? The best is both. Real magic comes when we use emotional/logical thinking. This is when we are using our whole brain and when we can come the closest to being a genius. The greatest discoveries have come about with this kind of thinking. Your truth will most likely come when you use your whole brain.

Taking the Bark Out of Dogma

Part of using our whole brain is to engage it emotionally and logically when we are looking at accepted truths. Just by saying they are accepted means that we no longer think about them and question their validity. Without questions, we are not thinking. Therefore, to be true to our search we must question everything or we are not truly searching or thinking.

In religion, "dogma" refers to agreed upon opinions amongst a group of people. Hence, Protestants, Catholics, Jews, Buddhists, Moslems and Hindus all have different dogmas.

Could the word, dogma, be used to describe beliefs in other parts of our society and culture? Is there an American dogma, a Democrat dogma, Republican dogma, patriot dogma or a business dogma? This is an interesting question because dogma is really agreed upon opinions and, in some cases, unproven ideas. No matter the passion of its adherents, they can be passionately wrong.

Recently, in business, we have seen many changes in belief and dogma. We have gone from the ideal of focus on one project to the ideal of multi-tasking. In the past, we have experienced an eight-hour day with coffee breaks and lunch---five days a week and now we do whatever it takes to get the job done even on our own time without extra pay. We have valued older experienced employees, as we should. Now we value younger lower wage employees, as we should. We have changed from loyalty to company and employees to loyalty to profits at all costs. We have moved from honor and honesty being the highest of ideals to a culture of spin doctoring, deniability, and cover-ups. Many are outraged by this, but believe it is OK as long as one is not caught. It will truly be interesting to see which business beliefs and dogma will survive the test of time.

Business theories come and go, some become fads and others advance to group belief as fact and as dogma. Nevertheless, they still remain as theories, ideas and beliefs and could be wrong! They are not facts, as many believe.

Ten-thousand MBA's, the Harvard Business School, Forbes and all the experts could agree on a dogma and be **WRONG! TRAGICALLY WRONG!**

Warren Buffet, billionaire, super successful businessman, financier and empire builder, hires mainly people who are over the age of fifty. They, along with Warren, built his business empire. You can't argue with his incredible success. This goes against the agreed upon dogma of only hiring younger executives. Of course, Warren has always been known for being a contrarian and he rarely goes along with conventional group thinking.

That is the point of these paragraphs. Open your mind to your own ideas, your own evaluations and your own inspiration. Reject group think—reject dogma and think for yourself. You have amazing intelligence. And who knows perhaps some ideas may come from your Higher Self.

In our quest for truth and light we owe it to ourselves to test all our past assumptions. When we were young, it was good to have our parents give us a foundation of beliefs to start our process for defining the world. But now as we have matured and found new knowledge, we find that the universe does not revolve around the planet Earth and Earth is not flat. We discover that the experts know very little and we have as much of a chance at discovery as anyone else. Reject popular opinions of the experts and find your own truth and your own light. They may be right but you are the one to make the judgment based on your own truths.

MYSTERY OF THE DARK SIDE
OR
WHY DO GOOD THINGS HAPPEN TO BAD PEOPLE?

Talking about truth and untruth we come to the idea of evil or the dark side—certainly an ally of lies and untruth.

George Lucas makes movies about the Dark Side. These films have fascinated moviegoers for over twenty years. He has taken a taboo subject (evil) and repackaged it in acceptable nonreligious terms. I am convinced if he had used the voice of the pulpit and said that Anakin Skywalker turned to evil and Satan then he would have lost his audience. This is why you don't hear most preachers talking about evil and Satan anymore—they don't want to lose their congregations.

There is a good reason why people don't want to talk about evil and Satan. Much evil has been done in the name of getting rid of evil. The Crusades, the Inquisition and witch burnings are good examples of doing evil to get rid of evil. No wonder people are turned off by these words. They have been used to manipulate people to do bad deeds since the dawn of history.

But why has Lucas captured so much interest in his movies and the Dark Side? Because this little talked about taboo subject, which affects all of us, can be talked about quite openly in his movies.

Anakin Skywalker's turn to the Dark Side of the Force happens quite innocently. He wants to protect the girl he loves. How ironic that love could be the inspiration for evil. We all are capable of going to the Dark Side when we are willing to hurt others for noble causes.

Those who we think of as the greatest embracers of the Dark Side, such as Hitler, Stalin, and unelected leaders, all thought they were doing good for their people. They thought they had to kill, enslave, and imprison many of their own minority citizens to do this "good." The executives at Enron thought they had to hurt their own employees and the citizens of California in order to do "good" for Enron.

Leaders who think they will gain the world if they sell their souls will only see the forfeiture of their soul, a temporary appearance of gaining the world and then a complete renege of the promised world. Good things happen to bad people for only a short time. Then, like the executives at Enron, they see their empire collapse overnight. The Dark Side may appear profitable but will always eventually lead to failure. Too many good people will not stand for evil.

How do we know if the Dark Side is tempting us? Here are a few key indicators.

- When we attack others instead of facing our own failures.

- When we don't take responsibility for our own lives.

- When we blame others for our life.

- When we are willing to hurt others for our own gain or the gain of those we love.

- When we are willing to tell lies to others and ourselves.

- When we stop being lovers of truth and people and start being lovers of fantasy and power.

Life is so much easier if we love people and truth.

HEAVEN AND HELL

So if good things happen to bad people temporarily, do they end up in hell or heaven eventually?

For the sake of argument, let's temporarily set aside the belief in the afterlife. Let's pretend that all our just rewards are here and now. Would many of the great religions of the world still be able to help us? Do they have practical advice for living our lives and finding true happiness right NOW? In other words, if we followed their advice can we predict if we will find Heaven or Hell in this life without having to wait for death and the afterlife?

Great minds have been contemplating the big questions for thousands of years. Some say they were inspired by God and so started a new religion. Others only saw themselves as philosophers trying to figure out what it is all about and how we can live the good life or the best life. Does it make sense to start our quest for answers by seeing what the sages have said down through the ages? It does, however we should include more than one sage.

There is one universal truth that has come to us from every major religion since the dawn of time. This truth gives us the keys to creating an exceptional life. It deals with human relations.

The Hindu holy books taught it 3,500 years ago.

This is the sum of duty: do not do to others what would cause pain if done to you.

— Mahabharata 5:1517 Bhagavad Gita

Zoroaster taught this truth 3,000 years ago to his fire-worshiping Persians.

Do not do unto others whatever is injurious to yourself.

— Shayast-na-Shayast 13.29

Buddha taught this truth 500 years before Christ on the banks of the Ganges River.

Treat not others in ways that you yourself would find hurtful.

— The Buddha, Udana-Varga 5.18 The Dhammapada

Confucius taught it 2,400 years ago in China.

One word which sums up the basis of all good conduct . . . loving kindness. Do not do to others what you do not want done to yourself.

— Confucius, Analects 15.23

Lao-Tse taught it to his Taoist disciples in the valley of the Han.

Regard your neighbor's gain as your own gain and your neighbor's loss as your own loss.

— T'ai Shang Kan Ying P'ien, 213-218 Tao Te Ching

The Judaic texts taught in the Torah.

What is hateful to you, do not do to your neighbor. This is the whole Torah; all the rest is commentary.

— Hillel, Talmud, Shabbath 31a Torah (The Law) • Nevi'im (The Prophets) • Ketuvim (The Writings)

The Prophet Muhammad taught this truth to his followers in the same part of the world as two other major religions.

Not one of you truly believes until you wish for others what you wish for yourself.

— The Prophet Muhammad, Hadith The Qur'an

And Jesus taught it to large crowds of common people in Judea 2,000 years ago.

Do unto others as you would have others do unto you.

— Jesus, Matthew 7:12 The Apocrypha • The New Testament

Yes, they all taught the Golden Rule. They taught a principal that is so simple that it is often ignored. Like most great wisdom, it tends to be so simple that most of us can't believe it has great worth. We seem to attach value to complexity. Please pay close attention, as this is a truth that can change your life. It is perhaps the one defining philosophy that will make the most difference. Whether you believe in a religion or not, this truth, which is recognized by all mankind from the beginning of time, will set you free and create a heaven on Earth. All one must do, is think of others as we think of ourselves. Show them an example of how you would like to be treated by giving them that love. It works whether you believe in a God or you are an atheist. Most religions believe this truth. Perhaps there is a reason why most religions talk about the Golden Rule. Perhaps it is because it works. Perhaps it is a great truth. You don't have to take my word for it. Start your own experiment.

As we go about our day and deal with people, our mind should be asking the question: "If I were the other person—how would I like to be treated?" If you are meeting people at a conference, would you like to have them look over your shoulder to see if there is someone better with whom to talk? Give people your full attention and full eye contact. Would you like people to be thinking of their answer to your comments without paying attention to what you are saying? Also, give people your full mental attention. Would you like people to criticize you publicly in writing? Talk to the person privately with as much compassion as you would like to receive if the roles were reversed. How do you think people would respond to your kindness? Do you think you would have fewer problems with people? Do you think your life might get better? Try it in your own life and see if it gets better. Try it in your business and see if word-of-mouth brings more customers. This concept works worldwide in all cultures, at all times in history, and it works no matter who you are. Start today—"Do unto others as you would have others do unto you."

Coming back to the original question of whether the teachings of philosophy and religion could help us here and now and not just in the afterlife, we find the answer. I think we would have to say with the above example of the Golden Rule--yes we can bring Heaven or Hell to our present situation. We can treat people well and have good treatment in return. Or, we can treat people with disrespect, coldness, and selfishness and reap the consequences. Generally the consequences are similar actions toward us. We are deserted and we live a lonely life. Children and friends abandon us. Study the masters, sages and philosophers to make your journey toward truth and light shorter.

MAKING YOUR LIFE PLAN IN SEARCH OF TRUTH

- ❖ **Find your current spiritual beliefs.** National Public Radio has recently reestablished an old radio program. It is called *This I Believe*. Famous and ordinary people read an essay they wrote about a kernel of wisdom that has guided their lives. This truth may have been obtained from the experience of living or any other source. Write your many *This I Believe* essays or just sentences. What are your truths and why do you believe them? Exhaust all your thinking until you are empty. It is important to know where you are before you create the map to find your destination.

- ❖ **Open your mind to all paths to truth.** As Plato observed everybody sees only part of the light and the rest is shadow. Some see more light than others. It is our job to find and search out these people and become one of them. There are many paths to truth and we need to honor those who are searching for that truth. Condemning others to Hell because they do not agree with us only closes our mind to possible truths and reality. The battle of religions is one where all participants lose.

- ❖ **Read and research all religions, philosophy, and all great thinkers.** Start from your beginnings. If you were brought up in a certain religion then learn about that religion inside and out. Now, if you were brought up protestant or catholic then learn about the teaching of the other church. Compare them with the one in which you were raised. Study other aspects of Christianity and its holy books. Study the older religions such as Hinduism and its holy books, Zoroaster and its teachings, Buddhism, Confucianism, Islam, Taoism and others. Even study New Age thoughts. Is your faith strong enough to look at other truths? Perhaps it is a good idea to let our faith grow and mature. As you study these religions it may make you think: " That is a new idea for me—I never thought about it that way before." These new ideas may resonate with you as profound truths. Also, you will find that there are more similarities to most religions than differences. This study may make your faith stronger. Next, study the philosophers. These people spent their lives trying to figure out how to live the best life, how to have the best society, the best friends, to think clearly and to describe reality. By reading them, we stand on the shoulders of giants and our perspective is enormous. Read biographies and especially autobiographies of great people. You will learn their truths and they may give you those "Ah-Hah" moments for your future success. Even great literature teaches great truths. Study it. Of course, also attend sermons, lectures, seminars, and classroom study. Listen to CD's and tapes in your car and subscribe to publications that deal with the important questions. If this all sounds daunting, remember you have all the rest of your life to study. It is never too early or too late to start your search for truth.

- ❖ **Keep a diary or journal of your spiritual journey.** You have already written down your truths above, however now you will keep track of your journey. Do you have stronger beliefs as a result of research? Do you have some new beliefs? Do you have even more questions? How will these truths change your actions in your life? The ultimate purpose of education is action. Are you taking action? Has your life changed? Where is your research leading—to a dead end or to a vast vista?

- ❖ **Meditate, contemplate, and look for answers from within.** I have a friend that tells his family and friends that he prays forty-five minutes three times a day. They know when he is not to be disturbed for he is in holy contemplation. It would almost be a blasphemy to interrupt this man while he prays. The truth is that he is not really praying 100% of the time. He is meditating, contemplating and hoping for wisdom to come to him from a Higher Source. Does it work for him? He is left alone to find incredible ideas. He says he does not know where they come from but he is rewarded with the most unbelievable, creative ideas that he has ever had. They have made a great impact on his life. He has written many groundbreaking books that have been best sellers on a worldwide basis. Now some people would say this man was wasting his time and lazy three times a day, but these periods of contemplation have been his most productive. Like this man, set aside time so that you have a chance to tap into wisdom and ideas that are just possibly coming from a Higher Source. When you drive to work, try it without the radio, CD's or tapes. Exercise without noise. Create a retreat in your home for contemplation. Be sure to write down any wonderful ideas, as they can be lost within a blink of an eye. They are as forgettable as dreams.

❖ **Have fun with your search**. Believe me, if you search for truth and light you will find truth and light. For some reason we are wired in such a way that it can be a delight to find truth. Just asking the questions, we seem to discover the hidden answers in the most unlikely of places. Most philosophers felt the highest joy a person could find was when he or she found the truth about reality. In the Western world, we are no longer taught this wisdom. Find out for yourself the joy of discovery. Your life is guaranteed to be exceptional when you search for truth.

Chapter 8

The Genius in All of Us—Mental Growth

Constant effort and frequent mistakes are the stepping-stones to genius.

**--Elbert Green Hubbard,
1856-1915
American philosopher and writer**

As diamonds cut diamonds, and one hone smoothes a second, all the parts of intellect are whetstones to each other; and genius, which is but the result of their mutual sharpening, is character, too.

**--Cyrus A. Bartol, 1813-1900
American clergyman, author and poet**

Every man who observes vigilantly, and resolves steadfastly, grows unconsciously into genius.

**--Edward Bulwer-Lytton, 1803–1873
British politician, novelist, and poet.**

Why You Should Make a Life-Plan for Mental Growth and Genius

SCIENTISTS are constantly amazed about new discoveries with regard to the human brain. It is the only organ that can completely change itself into a new brain over the course of our lives. It will grow new blood vessels, new pathways for neurons, and new patterns for genius thoughts. I don't know about you, but I take this as great news. We all can have a chance for it seems that we are the ones that control the growth. We can choose to create a designer brain for our goals or we can let the media create our brain. The choice is ours.

It used to be that people believed that the brain did not change. People thought that the IQ would stay the same for life. The truth is that it changes and we can become smarter or we can become less intelligent depending on if we use our brain. This is definitely one of those instances of "use it or lose it." However, in this case it is: use it and it will become better. Some have linked senility with the consistent disuse of the brain. Others have shown that with great use one becomes more and more intelligent. Even at 84, Voltaire, the great French philosopher, had no match in all of Europe for wit, logic, and genius.

Here are some examples of how the brain can grow and change. Our eyes, like cameras, project a picture to the back of our brain that is upside-down. If you have ever looked under the cloth of one of those old portrait cameras, you would see exactly what I am talking about. Like that camera, the eyes project the image upside-down. Our brain is so sophisticated that it compensates for this "wrong" image and it turns it right side up in our perception.

Some scientists* decided to conduct an experiment. They gave subjects special glasses that would turn everything upside-down. It took just two weeks for the brain to again compensate and turn everything right side up. That means that the brain had to grow new neurons, new pathways and new functions. Of course, when these poor subjects were not

---

* George Stratton (1896). Some preliminary experiments on vision without inversion of the retinal image. Psychological Review, 3, 611-617; George Stratton, (1897). Upright vision and the retinal image. Psychological Review, 4, 182-187

wearing the special glasses, everything looked upside-down. It took another two weeks for them to readjust back to normal vision.

In another example, there are people who have a neurological condition called synesthesia. Now most of us would say that any neurological condition must be bad. In this case, we would be wrong. Synesthesia is when a pathway forms between the sense of sound and sight. The people hear colors. Each note has a corresponding hue. A symphony can be a glorious waterfall of colors, weaving in and out with one another. This extra sense seems to help musicians and composers hear and see the beauty of good music. It also helps them see clashing colors in bad music in ways that we cannot hear. They become better performers and better composers. Nicolai Rimsky-Korsakov, Franz Liszt, and Alexander Scriabin, are some of the famous composers that appear to have had synesthesia.

We have two examples of the brain re-wiring itself to accommodate the individual. Most of us thought that the brain we were born with was the brain we had to keep. What if we could intentionally train our brain to re-wire itself so that we could go way beyond our own expectations? What if we could gain new talents, new insights and a new world? This awareness of being able to "grow" our brains could be the start of our next evolutionary step.

So, how do you get to Carnegie Hall? Practice, practice, practice! By practicing we are re-growing our brain so that we have better talent and a better sensitivity to the music. With practice we can re-grow our brains to become better at almost anything. With practice, we become a faster typists, better singers, better speakers, better parents and better leaders. Practice will make us better but only if we want to become better. If we work without trying to improve then we could calcify our brain into mediocrity.

What is the one skill or talent that could create the greatest impact on your life? What would it take to gain this skill or talent? Make this the year that you start re-growing your brain to gain that skill or talent. Create a program of practice, evaluation and more practice to grow those neurons.

THE #1 SUCCESS SECRET

When we practice, we are really making shortcuts to memory. The pianist that plays an entire concerto without printed music has so many shortcuts and memory enhancers that he or she is really able to free the mind of conscious memory and put his or her whole soul and emotions into the music. This is how we get world-class performances.

Memory is really a force of nature! The one thing that contributes to our happiness and success the most is how we choose our memories. Do you have a strategy for choosing your memories or do you just let your mind rule itself? Most have never heard that they can choose their response to memories.

It is well known that happy successful people tend to be optimistic, they look forward to new challenges, and they are loved by their friends, coworkers and customers. Why is that? I am sure these people have had pain and suffering in their lives. I am sure they could have just as easily ended up being cynics and negative with a life full of lost opportunities and misery. But they didn't, they chose happiness and a life of joy. You can too.

Let me say from the onset that I am in favor of retaining all our memories--good and bad. The good ones can inspire us and the bad ones can give us hidden gifts and teach us valuable lessons. It is how we add our emotions to the memories that gets us into trouble. Those who try to run from their bad memories may create false memories and delusions or anesthetize themselves with alcohol or drugs. The streets and mental hospitals are filled with these people. Some who don't go this far may just live a wasted life because they are paralyzed by their memories. They have had no strategies for enhancing positive memories.

The number one success secret is how successful we are at controlling and managing our memories. Our memories control our attitude. Our attitude controls our vision to see opportunities and dream great dreams. Our attitude gives us the energy to go forward with those opportunities and dreams. So you see, our memory strategy is everything-- it determines happiness and success.

The nature of living includes suffering. Everyone suffers and goes through pain and misery. But not everyone lets it ruin his or her life. In fact, some thrive and create excessive happiness and joy. The happy people are not those who have never suffered. They are not the ones who have lived a charmed life. They have, however, had a memory strategy.

What do I mean by a memory strategy? It is very simple. First, we must remember all that we can so that we learn from living. Second, we must be very careful in choosing which memories we will reinforce with emotion.

I know a woman who has been married for half a century and every time she has an argument with her husband, she brings up the fact that he bought her a coffeepot for their first Christmas when she did not drink coffee. She also states that he did not tell her about all his debts before they were married. This is what I call manufactured pain and, in this case, it was manufactured for fifty years. Another woman can't get over how she suffered the injustice of receiving an F as a student teacher preparing for her teaching certificate, just because she was grossly overweight. Her teaching career was destroyed by this one grade. I know a man who talks about his horrible, manipulative ex-wife and gets into a rage every time. I know several people who received poison pen letters from "loved ones" and they reopen those wounds afresh every time they re-read these letters. All these people manufactured pain and suffering in theirs and other's lives by reinforcing the old bad memories and reliving them with great emotion. This can only cripple us and lead to a life of misery. If the brain and subconscious thinks that the world is a bad place, believe me, because of this belief, it will create a future that is bad. If it thinks the world is good then it will create a good world. Our beliefs shape our futures.

If reliving our bad memories will lead to an unhappy life, what will happen if we relive our good memories with emotion? It will create confidence, expectation of good, optimism, and the emotional maturity and energy to face the world with vigor. It will remove all fear. In short, it will put the power into the positive and minimize the negative and give us a life of success and happiness. Perhaps we should re-read those old love letters, we should tell our friends about the best vacation we ever took, or we should make new memories that are positive so we can reinforce our perception of the good life when we reflect on the past.

By choosing our best memories and reinforcing those, we program our brain to believe in the good life and we command our subconscious to create a good life in the present.

Start today by becoming aware of which memories you are reliving and reinforcing. Find the gift and lessons in the negative memories and shelve them but don't forget them. Find the positive memories--focus on those memories and relive those memories and soon you will have many more to add to a long list of happiness.

Memory is the first habit where we can improve our brain. Our second is overcoming our blindness.

Scotoma—Our Blind Spots

Scotomas are literally blind spots in our eyesight. You have seen them. Some people call them floaters--those small grey spots that you can see floating in your eyesight when you put your eyes out of focus and just stare at the wall. What does that have to do with our discussion? Everything! In our larger life we have bigger scotomas.

Every minute of the day, our brains are processing millions and millions of bits of information. Like a Google search, which comes up with 358,000 pages, our brain must determine which information is important and which is trash. Does it pay attention to the sound of the air-conditioning as it cools the room? Does it pay attention to the flashing TV in the other room as we are in an animated discussion? Does it sometimes ignore the fact that we left the sprinkler going for five hours and we forgot to turn it off?

There is a story told about Christopher Columbus and his adventure in America. It seems that when his ships first came and dropped anchor in the beautiful islands of the Caribbean he was asked an unusual question. The "Indians" wanted to know where he came from. He pointed to the ships. They didn't understand. They asked again and again and he pointed again to the ships. Like a person from Missouri, the chief asked: "show me." He took him out to the ships and not until they got close to one of the ships could the chief see the ship. Nothing had prepared the natives for this reality. They had never seen a watercraft any bigger than a canoe. Therefore, their mind literally could not see the ships. They had huge scotomas when it came to Columbus' ships. Of course, when the chief got back to shore he could see the ships quite easily and he helped the others also see the ships. I find this story amazing. Our minds can blind us to the most important events of our lives. If we are not prepared to see new changes and be open to new possibilities then we, like the dinosaurs, may be startled by our own demise.

Do we have scotomas when it comes to our preconceived ideas about certain groups of people? Do we "see" them as their stereotypes? If so, then we don't see them at all—we see our own ideas of how we think we see them. This blind kind of thinking can cause racism, sexism, ageism and an unrealistic positive bias toward other groups. But what is worse is this scotoma causes us to miss out on opportunities to interact with people who could solve many of our own problems. This kind of scotoma impacts our lives negatively because we are rejecting or accepting others unfairly.

Scotomas that cause us to think negative thoughts about other groups are perhaps the main thing keeping mankind from creating a better world. On the other hand, we can have positive preconceived ideas about people. We may vote all our lives for people from a certain political party because we think that party best represents our views. We have a scotoma because we refuse to believe this party could be bad. We prefer closed eyes and continued blind voting. One day we may find that the parties have switched ideologies and that really the other party best represents our views. As a child, we may have been told to respect authority. However each person in authority can be good or bad. Our scotoma comes when we think they can only be good or only bad.

So, no mater if our scotoma is positive or negative it still causes us to have a warped view of reality. This warped view causes us to make poor decisions, which may cause pain in both ourselves and others. It is when we ignore evidence and take shortcuts in our thinking with preconceived ideas that we get into trouble. Ignoring evidence and going with these shortcuts gives us great scotomas. When we voluntarily blind ourselves to our world, we make wrong decisions and we create misery in our lives.

The bad news is that scotomas in the eye cannot be corrected. The good news is that scotomas in the brain can be corrected. We simply wake up and start using our brain instead of relying on lazy preconceived notions. We look at the evidence. You say that there is not enough evidence in most new situations and that is why you have used these shortcuts? Then take the recommendation of Emerson, treat people as if they are good until they prove otherwise.

Trust men and they will be true to you; treat them greatly, and they will show themselves great.

**--Ralph Waldo Emerson, 1803 - 1882,
Essays, First Series: Prudence, 1841**

MAKE THE SMALL STUFF--POSITIVE

Now, we have to realize that even if we have our minds totally open and have eliminated all prejudice and preconceived ideas, that the rest of the population may still be asleep. They may still be unfairly judging us on all kinds of small stuff. Even our name may paralyze some people into thinking foolish preconceived ideas.

As an example let's talk about names. What's your name? What's your child's name? What's your company's name? What's your product's name? Does it matter?

Marion Morrison was a macho-gun toting movie star. I don't know about you, but Marion is not a name I picture in this role. Perhaps that is why the Duke changed his name to John Wayne. Faith Plotkin is a futurist that concentrates on trends, especially for women. Now with a name like Faith Plotkin, I would imagine that she writes romance novels. Perhaps that is why she changed her name to Faith Popcorn.

Is it possible that strictly on the basis of names and how they cause others to have preconceived ideas, we can intentionally change or increase our chances for success? Would the Hula-Hoop have done as well if it had just been called the Hoop? "Hula" put fun in the name. "Popcorn" put energy in the name. "John" put familiarity in the name.

The right name can mean the difference between failure and success. What is surprising is that there have been studies that prove conclusively that the names we give our children can affect them in amazing ways.

Herbert Harari and John W. McDavid in their study "Name Stereotypes and Teachers' Expectations" In the

Journal of Educational Psychology 65 (1973): 222-225, gave essays to teachers to grade. The same essays would be given different author names. The idea was to see if the name on the paper influenced the grade. They stated: "More common names are regarded as generally more attractive, and they connote more favorable stereotypes. In contrast, the rare and unusual names are deemed less socially attractive and they connote negative stereotypes." The name David got the highest grade, then Michael, Elmer and Hubert. Recognize, the same papers were used—just different names. What are the implications of name stereotypes for the student's entire academic career and maybe his or her life?

You have heard the phrase that high expectations lead to high performance. If a name has a stereotype that causes teachers to have low expectations then can it affect people's lives in other fundamental ways?

Thomas Busse and Louisa Seraydarian of Temple University in their study "The Relationship Between First Name Desirability and School Readiness, IQ, and School Achievement" *Psychology in the Schools* 15 (1978): 297-302, found the same kind of relationship between desirable names and school achievement. But they did an additional comparison---they checked the relationship to IQ scores. They discovered a positive relationship between desirable names and high IQ. Can expectations and name stereotypes even affect IQ's?

My point is that names are one of the most important things we can give children, companies and products. The right name is worth a million dollars in your pocket or it can mean a lifetime of happiness. Give great thought to naming a company or a product or a person. Test the name for stereotypical thoughts that come to other people's minds. Create a name that makes them want to do business, be a friend or have a positive first impression.

Now, if a small thing like a name can have such a profound effect on our IQ, school grades or careers, what other small things could affect our brains and lives? If we dress for success are we more likely to have success? If we have a large vocabulary, are we more likely to be perceived as intelligent or as a "damn intellectual?"

All these small things are scotomas of others and the surprising thing is that we tend to believe what others think of us. Our IQ may reflect their opinion of our name. If we want an exceptional life, then we must strive to change the little things so that we see a positive reflection in others eyes. Our subconscious takes on others opinions of us as affirmations of our identity. We can isolate ourselves and say: "We don't care what others think." However, our subconscious does care. We create a positive view of ourselves from the reflection of others opinions. It helps to project a positive image so that we can receive a positive reflection. If no one had scotomas, all of this would be unnecessary.

FEELING NO EMOTIONAL PAIN

Wouldn't it be wonderful to make it so we could insolate ourselves from the pain caused by people with scotomas and prejudices? Perhaps not!

We must talk about emotional pain, as that is the number one stumbling block for most people when it comes to creating an exceptional life. It is not the pain that is the problem—it is the response to the pain that seems to destroy all their plans.

In the chapter on health, we discussed the crucial necessity of pain. Pain lets us know when there is a problem. It is a great communicator to which we pay close attention. The pain is saying: "FIX THIS PROBLEM NOW!" It is uncomfortable so we will do something about the problem. Pain tends to be a great motivation for procrastinators. Removing the symptoms of pain by fixing the problem is desirable. That is what we are supposed to do. Removing the symptoms of pain without trying to fix the problem leads to worse problems.

Escape from emotional pain seems to be in epidemic proportions throughout the developed world. Tranquilizers, alcohol, and mindless entertainment are all growth industries. Life is so painful that many want to just escape. Escape tends to make life even more painful. Pain is a persuasive communication that something is seriously wrong. If we ignore or block it then we risk catastrophic problems.

Do we avoid pain in our lives? Do we stay with a hated job because we will retire in only seven years? We could be dead by then. Are we unwilling to admit that there is a problem with our marriage? Has our health gone down hill and we still ignore the symptoms? Is Johnny having trouble learning to read and we are hoping he will grow out of it? Are we ignoring pain because it is too painful with which to deal? Are we taking too many tranquilizers because we can't face life's problems? Wishful thinking is not a strategy. Most problems won't go away with inaction—they will only get worse.

Pain is a call for action and we should listen to it and take action. Even corporations and governments tend to break this rule. It is not just important to the individual it is important to companies as well. Have we set our companies up to ignore or block pain? Who tells us when something is wrong? Our customers, employees, stockholders and vendors are our nerve endings. Do we listen to these people? Do we look at their letters and e-mails? Do we sometimes kill the messenger?

Many web sites have no phone numbers, no e-mail addresses, and no snail mail addresses. One recently lost me as a customer because their password software was not working and I could not log in. There was no way to tell them it was not working. I wonder how many customers they lost that day and they don't know why. They feel no pain and have corporate leprosy.

Employees are on the front lines and are usually the first to feel the pain from customers. How frustrated some must feel when the message is not allowed to go to the brain of senior management. Is good timely information rewarded or is the messenger killed? Some employees are demoted or fired for having a poor attitude and not being a team player? Positive thinking is a good thing and should be encouraged, but when a company is unhealthy and in pain, it should feel that pain and strive to correct the problem. Companies are made up of people and these people are really taking strategies to avoid emotional pain. Avoiding this emotional pain leads to ruined careers and ruined companies.

America has seen some major bankruptcies in the last few years. Some companies are suffering under a horrible disease by isolating themselves from pain. Secrecy is one way to eliminate the pain. If shareholders don't know the TRUE financials then they will not call for a change in management or sell their stock. If employees don't know the true financials then they won't withdraw their company shares from the pension plan or look for another job. If customers don't know that the cigarettes may kill them then they won't stop buying the product. However, secrecy only works in the short term. Eventually pain will catch up with the reality of the disease. Shareholders, employees and customers will always discover the truth. Unfortunately, by that time it can be too late because the disease may have become terminal.

There is strength in noting our pain and addressing our problems. There is weakness and a form of malignancy in ignoring our pain and covering it up with secrecy and drugs. The brain receives messages from all nerve endings feeling pain, warmth and joy. Those nerves are part of our nervous system and really part of our brain. Anything we do to short-circuit those nerves and reality actually is short-circuiting our intelligence. We are intentionally making ourselves stupid, less able to deal with the world. The alcoholic, drug addict and isolated CEO in his ivory tower are all stupid when it comes to awareness of the real world.

Note your pain and do something about solving the problem. It is a true path to the exceptional life.

SURPRISED BY JOY

We have talked about pain and the importance of letting ourselves feel pain so that we can solve important problems. It is understandable that there would be people who would want to avoid pain. After all, pain is not pleasant. But, believe it or not there are some people who will not allow themselves joy. To lead an exceptional life we must feel pain and joy. We must train our mind to accept both of these feelings.

C. S. Lewis wrote in his modern classic, *Surprised by Joy,* that he forgot the joy he had as a boy. He forgot how he used to feel. He forgot about the wonder and mystery he experienced everyday witnessing clouds, insects and dogs. He forgot about his joy of the imagination and creating his own world through writing, reading and play. He forgot about the joy of friendship, and being loved by parents. You see, when C. S. Lewis lost his mother, his father went into deep grief and sent the boy to a boarding school.

Boarding school pretty much made him forget about his "childish" joys. Maturity was equated with unhappiness, problems to solve and struggle. How many of us think in the same way?

I will not tell you how C. S. Lewis was surprised by joy from his youth in his adult years. I will not give away the ending of his book of how he rediscovered this exquisite joy that most of us only remember as children. You will have to read his book for yourself.

I will, however, point at some hints that may lead your thinking in the right direction. We are told in the Declaration of Independence that we have the right to pursue happiness. What a wonderful right to have!

However, the Declaration of Independence does not tell us how to subdue happiness and put it in a cage. We have the right to pursue happiness but we see no description of what happiness really looks like and we have no directions on how to obtain happiness once we do have a description. In addition, we don't know how to keep it once we find happiness. I link joy with happiness and feel that one cannot have happiness until that person has joy. Consequently, it is important to rediscover how we experienced joy when we were children and to build on those skills. What were our happiest times like as children? Write a description of those times in your journal.

Many believe that we must have a $60,000 car, a $250,000 boat and a $1,000,000 mansion to be happy. Find the happiest people you know and ask them, "Do you have an expensive car, a boat or a mansion?" It is possible they do, however I think you will find that most do not. So maybe Madison Avenue is incorrect, maybe "THINGS" don't make us happy. At least they don't make us happy for very long and they can complicate our lives.

Are there rich people who are happy? I would say yes, but not because they are rich but in spite of being rich. Are there poor people who are happy? Yes, but again, not because they are poor, but in spite of being poor. Perhaps joy and happiness have nothing to do with money.

What should we look for then if they have nothing to do with money? Remember and reflect back on your best joys as a child. Were there people involved? What were you doing and what were the people around you doing?

Forgetting ourselves and getting caught up in the play of life, making contributions to the other players and just having a love and passion for life will get us closer to real happiness and joy. But there is one more ingredient---you will find it in *Surprised by Joy*.

It is important to find what makes us happy and what brings about joy. Create a description of your happiness and joy. Make conscious decisions in your life where happiness combines with joy on a daily basis.

Enthusiasm

How can we prepare our mind to be the most creative, most intelligent and most joyful?

Do you have friends that are too "cool" to be enthusiastic about life? Are they so sophisticated that everything is met with a blasé response? When you enthusiastically tell them a story about your life, do they respond---"I am not surprised."? When they say "I am not surprised," do you get the feeling that they are really saying, I AM NOT AMUSED? Would you rather be with them or would you rather be with someone who has passion, enthusiasm and a zest for life? If you say the later, then you agree with most other people. The world values enthusiasm and passion. Impressionistic paintings could be called "enthusiastic" paintings. These paintings bring record prices at auctions. Passionate enthusiastic artists, dancers, singers, musicians, writers, athletes, chefs, leaders and people from everyday life seem to all live exceptional lives. It is almost like enthusiasm is the price one must pay to enter the world of a charmed life. But is it really a price or is it a way of thinking that can promote happiness? Being a sophisticated blasé person is not for you! Your best future lays in becoming the most enthusiastic person possible.

All children have enthusiasm. Your dull friends once had enthusiasm. How did they lose something, which they had at birth? Learning to walk, children fall down many times but never give up. It is inconceivable that a child would think, "Well, I have fallen down 253 times trying to learn to walk----I think I will just give up---What's the use?" The child is so enthusiastic with life that he or she will never give up. Life is wonderful and is worth celebrating with enthusiasm. All efforts for success are worth it because this world is wonderful and success is just around the corner. This must be what that child is thinking.

Through the years we all have failures. We all can get discouraged. We all fall down. Through the years we gain evidence for failure and pretty soon we can start giving up earlier and earlier. We are no longer like the child. In fact, we can become negative, jaded, and cynical. Notice I said, "can". Loss of enthusiasm is a disease that does not respect age; it can hit one at any age, young or old.

If you are over forty, you may think that there is age discrimination in the workplace. And perhaps there is age discrimination. I, however, believe that if there is age discrimination then it can be overcome with enthusiasm. When I was an executive recruiter (head hunter), I often saw the better-qualified candidate lose to the less qualified candidate that showed passion and enthusiasm. Most age discrimination is not about age. It is about enthusiasm. Many young people are just starting their lives and are greatly enthusiastic. Some older people have seen it all and are blasé and not enthusiastic. The young enthusiastic person gets the job. But the older person with great experience and also with great enthusiasm will many times beat the younger person with ONLY enthusiasm. Edison, Einstein, Buckminster Fuller and many more were noted for their enthusiasm throughout their lives. We can keep the enthusiasm of our childhood. Most churches recommend that one be like a child. Enthusiasm is the name of the game.

How can one gain back their enthusiasm? "Fake it till you make it." Act as if you are enthusiastic. Pretend that you love the sunset, exclaim with emotion, grab your spouse and hug him or her in glee. Act crazy like a child with happiness over great food, art and the idea of an adventuresome job opportunity. At first it will feel odd or like one is acting in a play. Then one day while you are "faking it till you make it," you will notice that you are sincerely enthusiastic. The act of smiling, and laughing and exclaiming with excitement affects your subconscious mind. You then are truly enthusiastic again and this brings magic into your life. You will have more friends, more opportunities, more promotions and MORE HAPPINESS. You will be leading an exceptional life.

AIMLESS DISTRACTION

So, we are enthused about life and we are on our way to creating a designer brain—we are confident our program is working. In fact, many around us also want to have an influence on our brains. Should we let them sabotage our program? Should we let them, in effect, design our brains.

I rarely watch TV because of the distractions of commercials. When I read books, listen to tapes, watch DVD's and videos, my focus is on something on which I choose to focus. Why do we believe companies have a right to a portion of our lives, unannounced, uninvited, to completely inappropriately interrupt our private lives? Anti-spam software is one of the fastest growing industries today. Norton Internet Security is constantly figuring out new ways to block ads, especially pop-up ads. Still the technology battles continue for the power and distraction of OUR thinking. Many states and the Federal Government are putting restrictions on companies that telemarket into our homes. Government is also clamping down on "junk" faxes. Billboards are illegal in many cities; and still the commercial distractions proliferate.

Our lives, where we are now, are a culmination of all our past decisions---especially those regarding other people. We make those decisions in the best way we know. We use our logic, our emotions, and thoughts to determine the next course of action. <u>Thoughts</u> determine our decisions. Change your thoughts and you change your decisions. Change your decisions and you change your life. William James said:

The greatest revolution in our generation is the discovery that human beings, by changing the inner attitudes of their minds, can change the outer aspects of their lives.

It occurs to me that if our thoughts determine our decisions and those decisions determine our lives then it is imperative to stay in control of our thoughts so that we do not lose control over our lives. Perhaps our ultimate freedom is determined by our thoughts and who controls them. Perhaps it is a good idea to receive salesmen and advertising by appointment ONLY. Your thoughts and your future are too important to be interrupted by aimless distractions.

We should clean our minds of unwelcome advertising. It takes up our time, it programs our subconscious in undesirable ways and it interrupts our thinking. This is thinking that could have made our lives better. Instead we let advertisers entice us think about Viagra and Coca Cola. We should be the ones that program our own subconscious. Propaganda and advertising are forms of molestation of the mind. Protect against them and control your own mind.

Making Your Life Plan For Mental Growth and Genius

- ❖ **Set up your health program to create a healthy brain.** Plenty of sleep, healthy diet and the right supplements go a long way toward making us think at our best. If a person does not feel well then they will tend not to think well.

- ❖ **Create a designer brain.** In your journal, make a list of all the skills, talents and information that would make you the perfect person to accomplish your goals. Do you need to know a foreign language, accounting, public speaking or leadership skills? Pick the most important one, which will have the most impact on your life and start <u>today</u>.

- ❖ **Create a plan to manage your memories.** Write down all your best memories. Why are they so good? How would you like to create a life with more good memories? Briefly look at your bad memories. Find the gift and lesson in each one. White down that lesson. Concentrate on the good memories and your future will be filled with new ones.

- ❖ **Find your scotomas—find your blind spots.** Become aware when you are making assumptions or prejudgments about people or situations. Use your journal to honestly numerate all of your beliefs that could be considered prejudice, sexist or presumptions about others. In the future, when you meet people whom you tend to prejudge instead look at them as if they are going to give you a great surprise. View this person as an exception to your scotoma rule. Assume people are good until they prove otherwise.

- ❖ **Program your subconscious by programming the small stuff.** Have you decided that you are going to become your own best hero or heroine? Play the role. Look the part. Fake it till you make it. Write in your journal all the small things you can change right now that would make you more resemble and act like the person you want to become. As you become closer to that person, others will affirm your new identity to your subconscious and you will actually make yourself into a new person.

❖ **Face reality whether it is pain or joy.** Use pain as an ally to information. Use it as an alarm or indicator to another problem. Solve that problem. Become a lover of reality and play the hand which you were dealt. Take control of your life and run with it for all it has to offer.

❖ **Find joy and happiness.** Write in your journal all the joys and happiness that you experienced in your childhood. Is there a common thread? Define what made you the most happy and joyful as a child. Now write what has made you the most happy and joyful as an adult. What is the difference between the childhood experiences and the adult experiences? Make a plan that will bring back some of those lost childhood joys. What do you think would create the most joy and happiness in your future? Take action on your plan and your thoughts.

❖ **Increase your enthusiasm.** Become a passionate enthusiastic person. Enthusiasm, passion and emotion are what fuel your dreams. It is also what gives others the motivation to give you a chance by financing your dreams. This is another "fake it till your make it" strategy. Get excited about good food, beautiful surroundings, or anything that is excellent. Show emotions and passions until they become your habits. You will find that as you enthusiastically appreciate good, more good will come into your life.

❖ **Eliminate all interruptions to your thinking.** Look at advertising only when you are shopping for a product or service. Surround yourself with an environment that is conductive to your goals.

Outside interruptions that take away from your goals should be minimized or eliminated.

- ❖ **Create your own home library.** Have a place of honor in your home for the tools that grow your mind. Books, tapes, CD's and other media pass information to your mind that changes it forever. This should be a sacred place, as this is where your future resides. You may also want to make this the place where you sit and write in your journal or diary. The importance of books goes without saying. Anyone who has achieved greatness was usually a reader. Of course, you already knew that—that is why you are reading right now.

For as the body without the spirit is dead, so faith without works is dead also.

James 2:26

The spirit is alive when we do good works.

Chapter 9

Legacy—a Different Kind of Immortality

Immortality lies not in the things you leave behind, but in the people your life has touched.

--Unknown

Cheese is milk's leap toward immortality.

**--Cliff Fadiman 1904-1999,
American editor, anthologist, and writer**

Act as if what you do makes a difference. It does.

**--William James 1842-1910,
Father of American Psychology**

Why You Should Make a Life-Plan for Making a Difference

WE come into this world as helpless babies wanting to be loved, wanting to be fed, wanting warmth, security and contentment. This is part of survival. Then we go through painful adolescence where we come to the realization that we don't just have to share our toys, now we genuinely want others to accept us and like us. We are confused because we are still ruled by the ego and still want someone to take care of us. But, we realize that there are others and perhaps if we want friends then life is not just about ourselves. From adolescence we grow into adults and now we know that life involves give and take with others. Temper tantrums are now frowned on even if you are the CEO. Again, we still have our ego and we still want to be loved and taken care of but now we think of loving someone else and taking care of someone else. We become self-sufficient and start providing everything that our parents used to provide. Shelter, security, food, warmth, love, and contentment become our main focus. Another way to put it is that house payments, car payments, credit card payments, jobs and happiness become our main focus. At least that is what we think we are working for and now we look to give those things in partnership to a spouse. Then the children come along and all of a sudden we are even thinking less of ourselves and thinking more about the children. We have come full cycle from our parents. This cycle ran from baby and caring only about the self; adolescence and realizing that there are others to care about; super caring or loving a spouse and providing a partnership to face the world; and now loving and caring for children who only care about themselves. Notice that the phases or stages of life involve a progressive increase in the caring or love of others. Also notice, that as we increase our love for others, we are thinking less about ourselves. In other words, there is less ego and more active love.

At least this is how it is supposed to happen. Let me say right now that age has nothing to do with whether or not one has reached the various stages. I have known quite a few adults that are still in the ego baby stage. Some are stuck in the adolescent stage and others are workaholics in the self-sufficient stage. Generally being stuck in the wrong stage at the wrong time can cause misery. Parents who are in the baby stage will have a dysfunctional family. If the parent only thinks about the self and ego, then it is hard to love the spouse or children.

Legacy—a Different Kind of Immortality

Most people are blind to the stages and have no idea that they should try to progress. The main reason people get stuck in various stages is that it is painful to grow and progress.

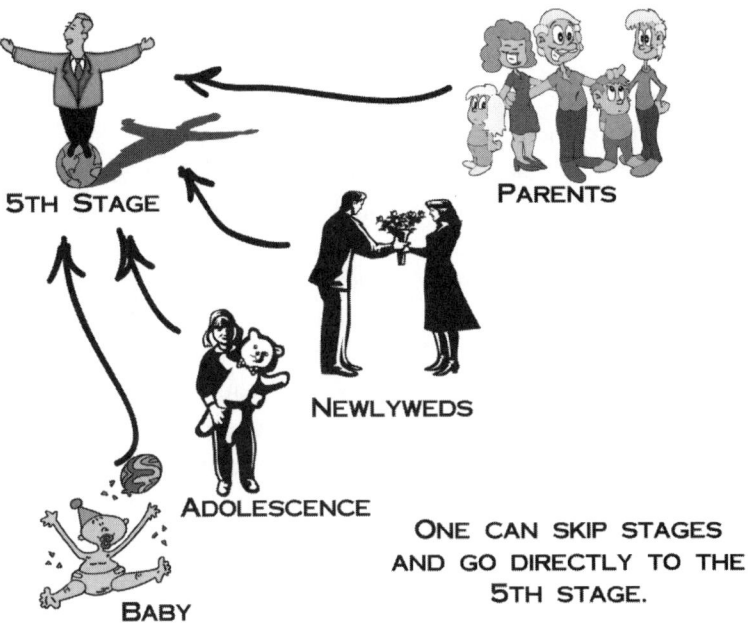

Adolescence is famous for the emotional pain. But each of the other stages of growth involves pain as well. It is very easy to sit back and be satisfied with oneself, especially if one is unaware that he or she could be better. Some people try to deaden the pain of growth with anti-depressants, alcohol and drugs. The key to growth and freedom resides in our mind. By deadening our mind we make the key so it will not unlock the door.

Could we be better? Is it possible that there is a fifth stage of life that comes after the adult stage and the parenting stage? Is there a stage that few talk about? Is perhaps this stage, the stage where we become full human beings at our very best? Should we try to reach this stage earlier? Or, can we learn multiple stages and live several at once?

People who do not have children or people who have seen their children leave home to start their lives may go through some of the pain that comes with growth. They start wondering whom they are going to take care of and whom are they going to give active love. Some buy a cat or dog and others turn to helping people outside of their immediate family. It seems that humans develop a fundamental need to be needed. Like the other stages, those that expand their caring and love to others will find that their ego is reduced further as their love increases to many more people. Empty nest parents may see that they no longer must care for children but must care for their own aging parents. There is definite pain in this kind of change as it causes one to switch roles. Aging parents don't always cooperate.

Those, like many of the isolated elderly, which stop caring for others will see their ego expand. They will find themselves slowly regressing back to the baby ego stage. We must keep caring for others or we regress back into children.

Ask yourself: What stage am I in right now? To summarize, we see the baby loving only itself, the adolescent loving a few friends, the newlywed loving the spouse, and the parents loving the children. Now we see the empty nest parents and the childless couple being inspired to take their love outside of the family and give it to the world in the form of service. As life has progressed, caring and loving has grown from a few recipients to many and we seem to gain increased joy by giving. Where are YOU now?

But do we have to wait until we have lived most of our life before we can enjoy stage five? The truth is, that we tend to alternate between stages during different parts of our life. In 1987, children from all over the world created the first international children's rain forest in Costa Rica. They raised all the money to protect, not just a few acres, but 56,800! Amazing, as it was done mainly with allowances and spare change. It is called *Bosque Eterno Do Los Niños.* You could say they were in stage five at the time. Children have started businesses that have made millions. Again they were not just in the ego stage, they progressed to the self-sufficient stage. The point is, that we can choose when we will enter each stage. We can choose a career or raison d'être that gives us balance where we can make the money for self-sufficiency, have time to love our spouse and children and have a product or service that helps thousands of people. We can fulfill the goals of all the stages if we are cognizant of them and take actions that will insure their success.

If we are to grow into exceptional human beings, then by the time we reach the end of life our focus should have changed. We are no longer as concerned with self as we are concerned with our contribution. Did we make a difference? Will we be remembered? How many people will be moved to come to our funeral? Does it matter? Is the world better because we lived? Hopefully, when we are on our deathbed we will look back over our life with satisfaction. Sure, we made some mistakes and may have some regrets. Everybody does. The crux of this chapter is that we create a life that is worth living and that is exceptional. And part of being exceptional is that we affect others by making their lives better.

Legacy is what is left over from our raison d'être when we leave this world. It can be either good or bad. We can leave a vacant lot full of weeds or a beautiful garden full of flowers.

Remember that rooster who gave its life to save all the other chickens? That rooster had a raison d'être to protect the flock. It gave its life to accomplish its significant purpose. When it died, that raison d'être turned into a legacy. The rest of the flock received life from the rooster's sacrifice. Sometimes our main legacy is simply to make life possible for our children or others. Being good parents, providers, and teachers provides a legacy that cannot be discounted.

Although supremely important, there are other legacies besides being parents.

GOOD OR BAD

A life spent making mistakes is not only more honorable, but more useful than a life spent doing nothing.

--George Bernard Shaw 1856 – 1950, Irish playwright

If our main purpose in life is like a good wine and it has "legs" then it will survive after us and the world will benefit from our life. But will we benefit from our living? Will we benefit and become better because we had flaws and were imperfect? Will we evolve into the kind of person that leaves legacies? Before we start judging ourselves and start getting stressed out about our legacy--let's rethink those judgments.

It is enough to come into this world, experience it fully, and then go out with a smile on your face. However, if we want an exceptional life, then perhaps we want to experience it more fully than most. If we are to "seize the day" then we must take risks and make mistakes. The more we judge ourselves, the more we will be risk adverse and so we will take fewer risks thus having a less fulfilling life.

So the secret to a fully experienced life is to condition ourselves to be resilient when we make mistakes. They will happen just as surely as all new skiers will fall. The skier gets up, shakes off the snow, knows that he or she will do better next time and so gets back on the ski lift. They don't scream, shout and cry about being a bad skier or a bad person. They simply try again. If only we could be as resilient when we make life mistakes. If only we could note our mistakes and how to correct them and not judge ourselves as either good or bad. Judging ourselves as good or bad is what makes us shut down. It makes us stop taking risks. If we don't judge, then we will be resilient like the skier.

But where do we judge ourselves the most? Our biggest risk happens when we reach out to other people. Our ego can be bruised when we are rejected or ignored. Remember how hard it was to ask for that first date or give that first speech? We were afraid of rejection. In grade school the other students may have laughed at our speech and we may have chosen never to give another. Fear of public speaking is only the second most dreaded fear—fear of death is the first. Equally, the cheerleader may have laughed and turned us down and we may have decided not to date in high school. Do you enjoy asking for a raise? How about justifying a raise? Aren't you afraid your boss may focus on you and you could come up lacking? Survival demanded that we have a fear of rejection, as any baby will die quickly without proper care. The problem comes when we have a crippling fear of rejection as a grown adult. Most people will not ask for raises and few bosses give them unless they are asked. Not a very good financial plan.

So, much of our success and an exceptional life really comes down to how resilient we are when we make mistakes. In particular, it comes down to how risk adverse we are when dealing with other people. Do we get angry, judge ourselves as not being worthy or do we optimistically go on to the next person and the next experience? Unless you are a hermit, you must deal with people. You can learn to love again. You can have more friends. You can see yourself as good and worthy of all the best relationships this world has to offer. Take more risks with people—they are worth it and so are you.

If our raison d'être is to turn into a legacy when we depart, then most likely that legacy will involve other people. Even if we have a life purpose to help animals, the environment or to clean up the oceans we will still have to deal with people. Ultimately, we can't get around the fact that whatever we do with our lives will affect people. A raison d'être that ignores people is a raison d'être that ignores reality. Everything on the planet involves people. Therefore it is paramount that we become skilled at loving people.

OUR FIRST LEGACY

We come into the world and hope that we progress to the point that we want to love others as well as our own family. We discover that we must take risks in relationships if we are to build a legacy that affects others. Really, what we have discovered, when you get right down to it, is that life is about people and relationships. That means life is about taking risks to form those relationships and doing what we can to give love.

Many cultures and religions believe that God is in each one of us; that there is a spark of divinity even in the lowest human being. In India, people meet total strangers and greet them by bowing and saying *namaste*: ("I see God within you.") This is a greeting of ultimate respect and one of giving blessings. Legacy is about blessing strangers and loved ones alike. Respect for strangers leads to trust and trust leads to advanced civilizations—even utopia. We could say that having a *namaste* attitude is one of the best legacies we can give the world. It leads to a better world. It also leads to better memories of those we leave behind.

The first legacy we give to others is their memories of us. What are your best memories? Do you remember friends in grade school? What about your favorite teacher—whom do you remember? Did somebody bless you when you needed it most? Did someone show you that you are of value? What are the best memories you had about grandparents and other relatives? Did you ever get introduced to someone and as part of the introduction you were given an unexpected compliment? How did that make you feel? Who else made you feel special and how did they accomplish this change? Were you taught to trust strangers? Did you go *Trick or Treating* in your neighborhood as a child? Did you believe that people were basically good? Write down your responses to these questions in your journal. From writing down those responses you will find how you are to respond to give others similar memories. What did you learn from the above positive examples? Write down your responses.

When we think back over our lives, the most important parts seem to be about people. Our fondest memories usually involve love and blessings. These memories were inspired by both the occasions on which we received blessings and those when we gave blessings. We realize that the giver and the receiver are both blessed. This legacy involves leaving good memories that will bless others throughout their lives.

Striving to create a character with the *namaste* attitude will put us in the right frame of mind to give blessings to others. These blessing are what make up positive memories. Positive memories will tend to influence others to have a *namaste* attitude and so the cycle will spiral up toward an exceptional legacy.

Having the *namaste* frame of mind will tend to make us all ask ourselves: What can I do to bless this person? What can I do to bless my child, my grandchild, my spouse, my neighbor, my coworker, people I meet informally like a waiter or waitress, people in my church, people in my club, and everybody else? What can I do to bless humanity? Think of what you can do. Do it. You will be remembered and you may change the world. Like the butterfly whose wing flutters could change the weather on the other side of the planet, your smile to a stranger may affect generations of people for a thousand years.

We don't have to build a multi-billion dollar company to change the world. All we need to do is create memories that change the way people think. Memories of love, cooperation and truth will create a world of love, cooperation and truth. A simple kind word and smile will leave an amazing legacy. It does not cost money but it changes lives.

Rut or Groove

Do we have a namaste attitude and are we leaving people with good memories? Are we at our greatest effectiveness for creating those memories? If we are going to live an exceptional life then it can't be done by being on "auto pilot," we must find how to be our best. How can we be at our best to create a raison d'être that has "legs" and that will turn into a legacy that will last for many years? How can we be at our maximum best to create those positive memories? It is important that we see clearly and look at our lives with an impartial attitude. However, it is next to impossible to be impartial. As long as we understand this, we have achieved a new kind of freedom. We know that sometimes we may be kidding ourselves when it comes to productivity.

For example, is your engine roaring and does your speedometer say you are going a hundred miles an hour but you really are just stationary spinning your wheels? Are you multitasking to oblivion but getting nowhere? Have you never worked so hard for so little return? Then you are in a rut and it's time to get into a groove.

A groove is when your speedometer says you are going a hundred miles an hour and you are! A groove happens when everything you do is going perfectly in a "natural one with the universe" way. You know in your heart and mind that things could not be better. You know that your contribution is making a difference and it seems effortless. When you are in a groove, you are doing what you should be doing at that point in time. Note that I said, "point in time." Timing has a lot to do with it. A groove is a slam-dunk in basketball, a hole-in-one in golf, and as the great choreographer Twyla Tharp says: it is when " . . . my dancers grab my ideas and abandon common sense." When they " . . . give something of their own and push everything to the edge." That is when we reach the state of perfect action. Scientists call this flow.

Legacy—a Different Kind of Immortality

Being in the groove is such a joyful experience that when we reach it, we never want to let it go. Bad policies and humdrum lives can develop from old grooves. That can be a problem. You see, we know that we are being totally effective and that we are using our mind, our intuition, and any other outside influences to create that perfect action, when we can feel the euphoria. There is a natural joy that penetrates our soul. We are using our total Being. That is what we are made to do. We want it to last forever. But like the unique snowflake that melts on contact with the nose, that groove is gone and a new one must be formed—a new snowflake must be formed. Time has changed, the world has changed and we have changed. We must constantly look for a NEW groove, a new song to sing, a new dance to dance, and a new poem to write. In business we must look for a new way to bring value, a new way to have employees add their groove, a new way to change the world. In life we must do the same. Systems, policies, and traditions tend to freeze the world in an old paradigm—the old grooves. They can contribute to ruts.

Old grooves become new ruts. The perfect way to do something last year may be the worst way to do it this year. The world changes but our tendency to love and hold onto those old ways never changes. We felt good when we were in the old groove. We miss that sparkle in our eyes. However, it is gone and denying that fact and setting up traditions and policies to support that fact will not bring it back.

Adventure out today to stretch yourself, examine your habits and routines, and do something new. As you go from a rut to a groove your joy will increase. This is one of the secrets to happiness. Get involved with the world and take risks. Our ultimate euphoria comes when we are in a groove and we are giving the world a legacy that is unique to us. Like the snowflake our gift to the world is completely different. For Twyla Tharp it has been unique dance, for Van Gogh unique painting and for Israel Kamakawiwo'ole unique singing. Find your euphoria, find your groove and find your uniqueness.

Another way of putting it is find your raison d'être and the more powerful your raison d'être the more powerful will be your legacy. You will know when you have found it when it feels like you are in a groove.

GOOGLE ME

Technology is famous for turning old grooves into new ruts. Many retail stores still use MS DOS on some of their computers. In fact, it does not take long for a new groove to turn into an old groove and then a rut. It can be a matter of just a few months.

Today technology has expanded the powers of the average individual to unprecedented levels. That is good news for you and me. At no other time in history has it been so easy to affect so many people at so low a cost. NOW it is easier than ever before to make a difference. If your raison d'être involves other people then you have a new powerful tool to make it happen and you have a new powerful tool to create a legacy. Businesses and organizations are already embracing this tool and now we are seeing individuals become famous overnight.

Let's talk about some of the new legacies that are being created.

An ordinary man in France single handedly convinced voters, through a blog, to vote against EU participation. He was not part of an organized political party, he was simply one individual with an idea.

Two graduate students decide to pool their knowledge and start a new kind of company. This new kind of company would empower customers, would let the customers drive decision making, would have a motto: "Don't Be Evil." This new company would be of the customer, by the customer, for the customer. Is it any wonder that Google has had phenomenal success? Is it any wonder that they were able to raise $1.2 billion in stock sales through an initial public offering (IPO)? This is perhaps the biggest business story of the decade. For a moment, let's look at the business world as it also pertains to the individual and how he or she will launch an exceptional life and a legacy. If you have not noticed, we have a revolution going on in the business world. The old guard still believes in top-down marketing. Most advertising is top-down marketing and it is very expensive. Management decides what, you the customer, will passively absorb through commercials, magazine and newspaper ads and radio spots. The trouble is, this kind of marketing is no longer working or effective. Newspapers and magazines are losing subscribers every day. People are using technology to eliminate TV commercials. Satellite radio and Ipods are offering music without radio spots. Top-down marketing is becoming less and less effective and big companies seem to be in a rut by doing what worked in the past. They don't understand what worked in the past is no longer valid. Multi-billion dollar companies are spending only $60,000 on a static web site while they spend millions on a TV commercial. Individuals who do not have millions to spend on TV commercials are taking on these big companies through the power of the Internet.

The companies that are seeing their businesses explode upward are the companies that are using bottom-up marketing. They sell to individuals one person at a time. The Internet makes it possible. There has never been a time in history like today where the individual can affect so many people by using the Internet. This gives us an unprecedented chance to leave a great legacy. With bottom-up marketing we make the assumption that customers are smart and have good ideas about what they want and what they will purchase. Bottom-up marketing has interactive web sites with discussion boards, blogs (web logs) and management asking for customers' advice on any improvements. With bottom-up marketing the customers feel that it is their company. They have an emotional investment that the company is part of their family and part of their lifestyle. Can you imagine life without Google or Ebay or Amazon.com?

One example would be, what advertisers have always known is the best kind of marketing, word-of-mouth marketing. Word-of-mouth marketing is really bottom-up marketing. Of course, this kind of marketing is a two edged sword. Bad products or services can be run out of business as people know the truth. Blogs or web logs are a powerful form of word-of-mouth. If you write a review of a bad restaurant experience on a popular web site then it may ruin thousands or millions of dollars spent in advertising by that restaurant. Written reviews on Amazon.com also create bottom-up marketing. Times have changed and the world is different.

Unfortunately, most people do not "Get It." They think they have no power if they don't have multimillion-dollar budgets for top down marketing. Top down is no longer the business or the political campaign model. Bottom-up is taking over! It is more responsive to stakeholders and makes it easy for customers to give suggestions or register complaints. All contact information including a feedback e-mail address, phone number and snail mail address are easily found on the web site of a good bottom-up company. All others are suspect.

Here is the good news. Because most people don't "get it," there is an incredible opportunity for those that embrace bottom-up marketing to do amazing things with their purpose and legacy. Few others will be competing using this method. Also, bottom-up people have the genius of thousands helping them be successful by their contribution to their endeavor. Most important, because the bottom-up person is working with thousands he or she has more of a chance to make a significant difference.

Embrace the Internet and bottom up marketing to give your legacy more power and more success. Embrace all technology that will give you leverage to your raison d'être.

Simple Legacy

Blogs (web logs) map an individual's thinking and ideas. They are a powerful way to use technology to get our ideas out to more people. Those ideas can become imbedded into our culture and thoughts just like any other kind of medium. With technology, perhaps a legacy is easier to give than we thought. What about pictures, videos, and diaries?

I have an ancestor who went to the Klondike during the Alaskan gold rush. He kept a fascinating journal. Another ancestor wrote about his experiences during the Civil War. Again a family treasure of another life lived. I have ancient pictures of stern looking ancestors who settled this great nation. You look into their eyes and wonder what were their passions, troubles and stories. I have a copy of a painting of Samuel McIntire (the great 18th century architect of Salem, MA,) another interesting relative.

I received a wonderful inheritance and legacy from all of these people. But it was not in the form of money or material gains. It was in the form of journals, pictures, and stories. With all my greed for more, I wish I knew more about my ancestors. I wish I had more of their journals, pictures and stories. I wish I could hear their voices in a recording or see them in a video. I wish I could know more about their struggles as I could put mine in better perspective.

It seems like there is an instinct or longing in each one of us to leave our mark, to prove that we were here or at least pass on a few lessons learned from a challenging life. However, many of us think that we must become famous and do great deeds to leave such a mark. That is not true, it is much easier than that.

Jim Rohn, the famous business philosopher, talks about his greatest assets. They are his journals, his pictures and his library. I am sure this man is a multi-millionaire and yet he feels that his bank accounts, stock certificates and deeds to real estate are of little value compared to his documented life of ideas; that the real value is in ideas, lessons learned and wisdom gained. These ideas made his successful life possible for Jim and he feels they are the most valuable legacy he can pass on to future generations.

All of us have learned from living and are still learning. This world is one big school and then we are assigned to a new classroom. Believe it or not, future generations will be interested in your life. Your life holds valuable lessons and should be documented. That is the whole principle behind books and libraries. We learn from those who came before us so we can take shortcuts to the good life and do not have to go through the same pain as our predecessors.

Write in your journal every day. Take lots of pictures everywhere you go. Write up your life lessons and tell your stories with audiotapes. Use video where you can and have an extensive library. These are the real treasures you will leave behind. These are a significant part of your legacy.

Making Your Life Plan to Create a Legacy

For many, the idea of creating a legacy can be a powerful incentive for success. We find the idea of a little immortality very seductive. It becomes another motivating factor or reason to become a fully actualized human being. It is another reason to do better, to go through difficult experiences and to go through the pain of growth. If we can make the world just a little better then we will find extreme satisfaction in the knowledge that we did, in fact, create a better reality. The following are some steps and exercises that will help organize some legacy thoughts.

❖ **Do you have a spouse and children? Do you have other family?** List in your journal how your influence on your family will create a lasting legacy for many generations. Create a legacy plan for your family.

❖ **Find your raison d'être and purpose in life.** The more powerful your purpose the more powerful your legacy. Make sure you follow the exercises in previous chapters to find your raison d'être. If you know what your raison d'être is, then write in your journal how that life purpose could leave a legacy for future generations. If you do not know your raison d'être then work it backwards. Think of legacies that you would love to leave behind. If you were to leave those legacies then what would be your raison d'être. Carnegie left a legacy of hundreds of libraries throughout the nation. Perhaps his raison d'être was to help people help themselves.

❖ **Be willing to take risks and make mistakes.** Nothing ventured—nothing gained. All great endeavors and legacies happened become someone was willing to take some risks and perhaps even lose everything. Life is not for the coward, for *a coward dies a thousand deaths, the brave just one.*

❖ **Life is for the believer in prosperity and abundance.** There is always more prosperity and more abundance for those who are willing to believe in it to such an extent that they are willing to give it away. Creating a legacy will create more abundance but it will also make the person incredibly lucky. It is worth taking the risks.

❖ **Be conscious that you are creating memories. You are an incredible influence on everyone you meet.**

Make the world a better place. Fill it with good memories. For most, that is the only legacy they will create. People's memory of you is your legacy, your gift. Make that gift one of love.

❖ **Constantly question life. Question whether you are in a rut or a groove.** When did you last feel like everything was going perfect and you were definitely at your best? How did that feel? What can you do now to get back into a groove and out of a rut? Write into your journal, not just about your job, but about all aspects of your life. Define how to be your best in every facet of your life. List your life roles: father, mother, sister, brother, employee, employer, friend, club officer, etc. Under each, list how you would like to be in a groove with that role. Being exceptional will create an exceptional life and an exceptional legacy. We can only be exceptional on a minute-by-minute basis through our roles.

❖ **Use all relevant technology and tools to expand your powers for your raison d'être and legacy.** Today technology is moving so fast that the average person finds it hard to keep up with all new developments. Some technology is so life changing that what was impossible last year suddenly becomes quite possible. Subscribe to magazines that discuss new technology. Your impossible dream may be very close to reality—unless of course you don't keep up-to-date.

❖ **Document your life with journals, pictures, tapes and video.** This is one of the simplest legacies you can give. Believe it or not, both your family and people hundreds of years from now will find it most valuable. Your struggle, joys and sorrows are of interest to many people. Perhaps your life can help them live theirs.

* **For a true feeling of legacy, read the story** *The Man Who Planted Trees* **by Jean Gono and apply the lessons.** It is a story about a man at age fifty-five, who has lost his wife and only son. He travels to Provence, in southeastern France, to live a very simple happy life. He lives alone with his thirty sheep and a dog. Each day as he watches the sheep, he plants a hundred acorns. This is in 1911 and the region is a virtual desert from the charcoal burners cutting down all the trees to make their charcoal. The winds blow, the towns are deserted and there is very little water. In thirty years, Elzéeard Bouffier plants over a million trees, revitalizes the region, causes the dried up streams from Roman times to run again, and creates a paradise for ten thousand new families. His only reward was happiness. We hear that truth inspires fiction. In this case fiction inspired truth. Provence has an extensive tree-planting program as a result of this story.

Elzéeard Bouffier reminds me of the true story of America's legend, Johnny Appleseed. To get the greatest leverage on our legacy we must choose a legacy that is like a seed in that it can, on its own, grow into a mighty oak. What can you put very little effort into (like planting one acorn) and then watch it grow on its own? Perhaps planting trees in your own community makes some sense.

By the way, I am surprised no one has planted another redwood forest outside of California. It seems to me, that these trees are so magnificent that they should not just exist in one place in the world. Another idea along these lines would include making manmade reefs off our coasts to increase ocean life. Wherever we can increase and improve life for all species, we increase and improve life for humans. That is what legacy is all about.

Chapter 10

Living—A Work in Progress

The shoe that fits one person pinches another; there is no recipe for living that suits all cases.

--Carl Jung, 1875 - 1961
Swiss psychiatrist

Get busy living, or get busy dying.

--Stephen King, 1947—
Prolific American author

Happiness is the reward we get for living to the highest right we know.

--Richard Bach, 1936—
American author

Don't brood. Get on with living and loving. You don't have forever.

--Leo Buscaglia, 1924 – 1998
American professor and author

Some Conclusions on the Exceptional Life

THERE are a thousand ways to an exceptional life but only one that is perfect for your life. Search your heart for the answers and they will most assuredly come. Most only respond to life instead of shaping life and making it into a piece of art. With the passion of an artist and the energy of a volcano, you will make your life exceptional. The question is—when? When will you start on the life you were meant to live?

DELAYED DREAMS *Recalling some of Chapter 2*

Most of us tend to put off our dreams. Why is that?

I was giving a presentation some time back and I asked the audience: "How many of you never found out what you wanted to be when you grew up?" Eighty percent of the audience raised their hands. They ranged in age from 20 to 60. So, it was not just young people starting out in their careers. Why have they not figured out what they want to be when they grew up? I think they may know what they would **REALLY** like to do but they have pushed that possibility to the back of their minds and have not given themselves permission to pursue this dream, this raison d'être, this reason for being, this purpose or this calling. They have been their own worst enemy in their own pursuit of happiness.

Let's talk about the most common myths and misconceptions that most people believe. These beliefs cause them to give up on their dreams.

If we were born to live a certain kind of life—a life with a well defined purpose or to live our raison d'être, then it is only logical to believe that it is possible to succeed at living that special life. A bird is meant to fly but I'll bet he has plenty of fear just before he is pushed from the nest. In fact, if he were like many people, he would never leave the nest just to be safe. These people fall into a trap of fear, doubt and misconceptions that cause them to give up on their dreams and live a life of regret and misery. Here are common fears and misconceptions that keep many from soaring like eagles:

❖ Fearing that money and passion do not go together. Fearing that if we go for what we really care about we will end up broke. The opposite is true. When we have passion for what we are doing, we put incredible energy and creativity into our dream. This is what it takes to become world class and exceptional. These people tend to be well rewarded.

❖ Fear that once we decide to go for our raison d'être there will be no turning back and all future possibilities will be limited. Untrue! It will give you more options because you have more experience and vision. Also, you can always change your mind when you have better, newer information. Remember there are no wasted experiences and all experiences lead to your purpose.

❖ Fear of not being able to clearly see the future and see definable goals. Whether you go for your purpose in life or you don't go for your purpose you will not be able to foresee the future. Goals are only approximates, best guesses and, although important, not mandatory for starting a better life. Sometimes it is just better to start and know that the future and goals will reveal themselves when appropriate.

The best-laid plans of mice and men often go awry.
--Robert Burns, 1759-1796
Scottish Poet

❖ A fear that everyone you know will stop loving you because you will change and become a different person. This is unlikely and perhaps an excuse for not going for your purpose in life. It is more likely that more people will like and love you than before because you are your authentic self. It is when we try to change ourselves to fit other's expectations that we end up having people treat us with indifference and we become miserable because we don't even love ourselves. When we become our authentic self we move from being like an ordinary piece of chocolate to becoming an intensely flavored piece of the best Swiss chocolate you ever tasted. If you love chocolate you will love this person more intensely. If you dislike chocolate then you will dislike this person more intensely. Some people don't like chocolate. That does not mean we should try to be a different flavor just for their sakes.

❖ The belief and misconception that we can't begin our life until we have a precise correct answer that tells us exactly what we must do. The idea that if we don't know our raison d'être then we can't begin. UNTRUE!

Using your journal and keeping your eyes and ears wide open, you can find the answers by living, by thinking, by journaling, by dreaming, by meditating, by praying, and by making mistakes. The important thing is to start. Don't start today—start this minute!

Mendacity

But are we being true to others and ourselves? This is a crucial question. When we start making and creating the exceptional life, it is essential not to live in a fantasy world. We must see reality with a crystal clear perspective. Our literature and institutions are filled with people who have lived a life of tragedy and lies.

For example, lies and liars, were the people Brick was so disgusted with when he was having his heart to heart with Big Daddy. Tennessee Williams brought home a topic in his poignant play, *Cat on a Hot Tin Roof,* which is rarely discussed.

The play takes place in the South and its subject is mendacity. Mendacity is when people create an environment of lies, petty lies, big lies and all other kinds of falsehoods designed to manipulate other's thinking. These lies eventually create a poison that makes everyone ill.

Cat on a Hot Tin Roof is a tragedy, a comedy and a lesson in wisdom for all of us. Williams shows how lives and families can be ruined through relationships of pretense. These are relationships that are built on false good manners without any show of our genuine selves.

Many people would say that Tennessee Williams was showing how Southern people hide behind good manners to avoid confrontation and real community. These people would be wrong. The problem exists in all parts of the country. It is not just limited to the South. It exists everywhere and we need to be aware of how we create false community or mendacity, as Williams would say.

Big Daddy talks about church and the special friendliness that does not extend outside the church. He talks about clubs where people act with their club persona—not their real self.

The play's main tragedy is that every character is really only concerned about themselves. They become mendacious just to manipulate others for their own gains. We really could say it was a play about love withheld and the exploitation of others to receive love, money and prestige.

The greatest gift we can give anyone is the gift of being our true selves. It is really a gift of love. But to be genuine, we must show our warts, flaws and controversial opinions. It also means that we must show our wonderful selves. This is the goodness or light that we take out from under a bushel. When we show our wonderful selves we tend to make some people jealous and angry. They feel inadequate because they don't think they are allowed to show their wonderful selves. When we show our flaws we tend to make these same people happy and willing to gossip. No matter what we do these people will not be our friends—ignore them.

It is our job, indeed, our duty to live our lives with complete veracity—complete truthfulness. We will have better marriages, better friendships, and better relationships with whomever we come in contact. Become a compulsive truth teller. Although it may cause some people to be upset, in the long run they will trust you and know exactly where you stand.

The best part of living a life of veracity is that if we are true to others then we will tend to be true to ourselves. When we lie to others, then we tend to lie to ourselves—this leads to insanity. When you think about it, if being our true selves is a gift and a way to show love to others then it is also a gift and a way to show love to ourselves.

The accuracy of our truth to others and ourselves will determine our response to this perceived reality. It will also determine other's response to our testimony. And because both our own and other's actions may come as a result of our view of reality, our view will thus determine our future.

Stop the mendacity—start the veracity on your way to an exceptional life—your future depends on it.

CELEBRATING SUCCESS—OR FAILURE

One thing is for sure—if we stretch, if we run and if we try new things, we will fall and may fail. We will want to own up to these "failures" both to ourselves and others. Mendacity is not for us. One could say that falling and failure are symptoms of future success. What is important is how we view falling and failure.

Leo Buscaglia, the best selling author of *Living, Loving & Learning*, tells the story of little Johnny. Little Johnny did poorly in school. On his last test he got eight out of ten questions wrong. Buscaglia asked why do teachers count how many we get wrong instead of how many we get right? He says, why not say to Johnny—"JOHNNY, YOU GOT TWO RIGHT---BRAVOOOOOO!!!"

There is a custom in Italy that confuses a lot of Americans. In Italy, when you sit down at a table in a restaurant, that table belongs to you for the whole day if you so choose. You will see many people drink espresso and read books for hours on end. This does not bother the waiters for it is your right to stay as long as you like. In fact, it is considered very rude for a waiter to bring you your check unless you have made a request. Many Americans just keep sitting at the table waiting for the check and it never comes because they did not ask for the check. A good phrase to learn is "*Il conto, per favore*"—The bill, please.

After an incredible two-hour meal, my wife and I were ready to go. I looked over at our waiter and he came up to me knowing that my Italian was pitiful. In rapid Italian he asked me if I wanted the check. The only word I understood was "*conto*". So I answered "Si." He did not think this American would understand one word and was amazed and shouted BRAVO. Have you ever been "bravoed?" I was so happy with these wonderful Italians I wanted to study hard and learn their language. He celebrated my limited success.

It occurs to me that when we celebrate even small amounts of progress that we give energy to more progress. On the other side of the coin, when we bemoan small and large amounts of failure we are then celebrating failure and giving energy to more failure. Cheerleaders never comment on missed free throws, lost opportunities or missed baskets. They cheer stolen balls, rebounds, and, yes, points earned. But note that they also cheer all actions that lead to scoring. Not just scoring.

The salesman many times only earns praise when he or she sells something. Sales managers need to also celebrate those actions that lead to sales—more new appointments, more returned calls and better use of time.

The job hunter should not just celebrate when he or she gets a new job. Scheduling new networking appointments, meeting more people and making the résumé sharper should also be reasons for celebration.

We should, however, all guard against celebrating failure. Celebrating eight wrong answers instead of two right ones will lead to more wrong answers. Celebrating low sales and no job instead of celebrating more appointments and networking progress will not energize success.

What do you want? Celebrate what leads to that! Do you want an exceptional life? What is your personal definition of an exceptional life? What do you need to do to bring about your exceptional life? Celebrate each step of progress toward your exceptional life. This will give you the energy to walk through fire so that you can accomplish your next goal.

SUCCESS TO SIGNIFICANCE

While celebrating success is necessary to insure additional success, can we take it too far? Do we need to have moderation in all things including the celebration of success?

Once we start seeing that we are living our dreams and we are bringing about an exceptional life, we can start thinking that we are pretty good. In fact, we can think we are so good that we will allow our egos to start eating our brains. This is not for you.

I am privileged to know a lot of professional speakers. Many of these people are incredible examples for the rest of us. They live the highest ideals and are always searching for new ways to serve their audience. The best are humble down-to-earth people with high self-esteem and high self-confidence with no need for ego stroking. These people not only can gain success but also gain significance.

I also know the other kind of professional speaker. I must say that the speaking profession carries a high risk to those who do not have a solid understanding of their true identity. These people can become addicted to the applause, the limelight and the fan adulation. They frequently seek compliments, honors and prestige. Their addiction requires that they must be constantly reaffirmed by their audience and all with whom they come into contact. If they do not get it they have withdrawal symptoms of rudeness, arrogance and snobbishness. These people can gain success but rarely gain significance.

The first group of speakers is focused on the message and the audience. The second group of speakers is focused on themselves and how the world relates to them. In other words, if we focus on ourselves exclusively we may gain success but will rarely create a lasting contribution that will be significant to the world.

This principle is not exclusive to professional speakers. It applies to all walks of life.

There are two types of leaders. One type creates followers and the other creates leaders. The leader that creates followers may create success for a limited time period but will not create a lasting significance. The difference again is focus---either self or others.

The leader that focuses on self creates followers. This leader can be autocratic, wants no reports of bad news and will slash and burn employees until an organization is created that revolves around his or her magnificence. This person's ego wants to be worshiped. He or she can create a success that is impressive but short-lived. Alexander the Great conquered the known world. When he died the empire disintegrated. I am sure you can think of many in the business world who had a dramatic rise to power and then fell.

The leader that creates more leaders creates an organization that has no boundaries. It is not limited to one person's ego. This leader focuses on ideals and ways to improve the world. They capture the imagination of the best and they employ the best. These people are self-confident and humble. They do not seek publicity or honors. They seek the creation of significance. In my opinion, some examples would be George Washington, Abraham Lincoln, Winston Churchill, Mother Teresa and Mahatma Gandhi. Among business leaders it would be Darwin Smith of Kimberly-Clark, Colman Mockler of Gillette, Alan Wurtzel of Circuit City, Cork Walgreen of Walgreens, David Maxwell of Fannie Mae and Dick Cooley of Wells Fargo. My guess would be that most have not heard of these business leaders. This list of leaders came from a study that was done for the book *Good to Great* by Jim Collins. It is interesting to see how well their companies performed in the stock market.

> *The good-to-great examples that made the final cut into the study attained extraordinary results, averaging cumulative stock returns 6.9 times the general market in the fifteen years following their transition points. To put that in perspective, General Electric (considered by many to be the best-led company in America at the end of the twentieth century) outperformed the market by 2.8 times over the fifteen years 1985 to 2000.*

The reason you may not know these names is because these people were building companies not egos. Even on a personal level we can see a difference between success and significance. Did we marry because someone loved us or because we loved him or her? Do we have children so we will have little people who love us and worship us like gods or do we have children because we want to love children?

The real question is, are we living our lives in the constant pursuit of worshipping our ego and ourselves or have we found a higher purpose that goes beyond ourselves---a purpose that can fire our imagination and all around us? Exceptional lives put the ego aside for higher goals.

STRANGE PRACTICES

While we are wondering if we are letting our ego eat our brain, one of the indicators of brain nibbling is our level of compassion. As a rule of thumb, high compassion equals less ego and low compassion equals high ego. As Rome burned and Nero played his violin, there is no question this man had a big ego and low compassion.

Our culture sometimes mistakenly defines compassion as weakness. Would we ever give compassion to our competitor, employee or union negotiator? Compassion is one of the ingredients to a happy exceptional life. Let me tell you a story about some of the strongest people in the world and their compassion.

Kill a lion—become a man. The Masai tribe of East Africa and Kenya has some unusual traditions. A young man, or really a boy, must prove himself by being sent into the wild with only a spear and his own wits and bring back a dead lion. When he does this he is welcomed into the brotherhood with the other men. The Masai men do not lack courage and are ready to face their fears. Some would call them macho.

The Masai are some of the tallest people in the world many measuring over seven feet in height. They are nomadic and mainly subsist on the blood of their cattle. They open a vein, drain out a pint and the cow goes on living and feeding. Doctors have been amazed because this is a super high cholesterol diet. Yet the Masai's own blood measures out as having low cholesterol. Perhaps the fact that they run many miles each day may offset cholesterol in the diet.

I have a friend who lived with the Masai while he worked for the CIA. We could not get him to tell us any secrets, however he did tell us some amazing things about the Masai. One story I will never forget. One day a man lost his wife. The man, understandably, went into great depression and mourning. In the Masai culture it is OK for men to weep.

It is OK for these lion killers—these cow vampires—these macho men to cry. But it is also OK to give compassion and comfort to your "brother" who has lost his wife. Did they say to him "I am sorry, here is your condolence card?" NO! Did they expect him to snap out of it in a few days? NO! Instead they did something different, which we can all learn from.

About eight families live in each nomadic group. All the men, including my friend, came to the mourning man and put him on the back of one of the men. Then as a group, as the man was crying, his "brothers" carried him and they started off running silently through the countryside. They continued to run and run and run switching the crying man from one man's back to the next. They ran all night and well into the next day. All of this man's male friends carried him in his grief. These macho men gave their brother what he needed, compassion, comfort and love.

When I look at this so-called primitive culture and how they take care of those with grief I have to wonder which is the primitive culture, the Masai or the United States? How could we be more compassionate? Look at the strong bond these men must have.

Can you imagine what a few people with this kind of bond could do if they had a common purpose—a common raison d'être? The Masai thrive under harsh conditions. This common bond built on community and compassion is what it takes for a group of people to do extraordinary things. Your raison d'être will require you to join with others for common purpose. Build community, build compassion and you will have no trouble finding dedicated associates.

CONCLUSION

We have come a long way through all these chapters. The exceptional life is worth the effort and the journey. After all, what else do you have to do except live? You might as well spend the time making that life exceptional—the other kind is just not as much fun.

Read through each of the chapters again and make sure you do the exercises. *As* Leo Buscaglia says: *Don't brood. Get on with living and loving. You don't have forever.*

Here are a few conclusions:

❖ **Our raison d'être is the most important thing we can find out about ourselves. Dedicating our life to our purpose or raison d'être is more than half the battle to an exceptional life.**

❖ **One is lost until one loves. Everyone is searching for love. They would be better off if they just gave love without any expectations, then they would have more love than they could handle.**

❖ **It is healthy to be responsible for one's health. Become your own health expert—it could save your life.**

❖ **Money and wealth are more in the mind than in the wallet. Create a** wealth consciousness and the money will come.

- ❖ Use the most advanced computer on the planet to plan your life. Use your mind. Without goals and plans—nothing happens.

- ❖ Search out truth throughout your life. When you think you have the answers you may be more ignorant than your realize. Life is meant to be explored, sampled and experimented with every day. You are a witness to your life. What is your truth?

- ❖ If your mind is not growing then it is decaying. The greatest among us have grown their minds throughout their lives. That is why education is a lifelong practice.

- ❖ It could be that our legacy is our raison d'être. I know that most raison d'êtres leave a legacy. Use the power of legacy and what you will leave the world to energize your raison d'être.

You are a hero or heroine for your own life and maybe others. Going for your exceptional life will change your life and perhaps the world. The world needs people like you. Live your purpose and we all benefit. Help others to live their purpose and we all benefit. You were meant to make a difference. Live your purpose.

Twenty years from now you will be more disappointed by the things that you didn't do than by the ones you did do. So, throw off the bowlines. Sail away from the safe harbor. Catch the trade winds in your sails. Explore. Dream. Discover.

--Mark Twain, 1835 – 1910
American Humorist

Afterword

OUR thoughts direct our actions. Our actions create a life. With the right thoughts and their resultant actions you will create an exceptional life. It is hoped that this book will spawn those thoughts and actions. Whether our actions are right or wrong, it is better to take a wrong action than no action. The right ones will be rewarded and repeated and the wrong ones will teach us through discomfort. That is the tuition we pay to the school of hard knocks. Hopefully this book teaches the right actions and will be a shortcut to rewards. The important thing is to be awake, to think and to take action. Right or wrong, action is better than no action. Start your raison d'être plan, your love plan, your health plan, your wealth and prosperity plan, your goal planning life plan, your search for truth plan, your plan for mental growth and genius, and your legacy plan. Working in all these areas will assuredly create an exceptional life.

Now, you are the person of power. It is up to you to tap into that power and take the next step. As you take that step and grab hold of life, making it exceptional, refer back to this book. Let me know all about your experiences. How could the book be improved? Tell me your stories to illustrate important success concepts. When your life does become exceptional, celebrate and please send me a symbol of that life. If you write a book, send me an autographed copy. If you build 50' yachts—well you know what to do.

May you live the life you were meant to live—L'Chiam!

Best wishes,
Kurt DuNard

EXCEPTIONAL Life Coaches are consultants who work with individuals and organizations to achieve the breakthroughs necessary to bring about success. Somewhere in our subconscious we have all the right answers. Exceptional life Coaches help us find those answers through questions and ready resources.

Contact Coaching@DuNard.com for a referral to a certified Exceptional Life Coach.

Appendix A

Your Exceptional Life Calendar

WHAT TO DO

Start

Raison d'être

Love

Health

Wealth & Prosperity

Goal Planning

Truth

Mental Growth

Legacy

Continue

Your Exceptional Life Calendar

IT would be easy to say that we need to do everything in this book all at the same time. Everything seems to be of the utmost importance. Like money, we don't have unlimited time and only Bill Gates has unlimited money. We must make priorities. This appendix attempts to set those time priorities, however you may wish to alter them. You have the final say and you have the best information on your life. With some kind of structure and plan few become overwhelmed with the immensity of the project. Tweak this list and come up with your own calendar.

Start—Doing it NOW!
Chapter 1 for more detail

- ☐ Buy a good journal that you will be proud to use.
- ☐ Make a list of all your priorities in your life at this time. What can you do today? What is most important?
- ☐ Make a list of all the rewards for an exceptional life. Make a list of all the pain and waste caused by living a life without purpose.

Raison d'être—Self Inspection.
Chapter 2 for more detail.

- ☐ List your gifts and talents.
- ☐ List the important experiences in your life. Why are they important?
- ☐ List your areas of knowledge.
- ☐ Who are your heroes—fiction and nonfiction. Why?

Appendix A
Your Exceptional Life Calendar

- ☐ Each night, write down a different question whose answer will make your life exceptional.
- ☐ Each morning write down your subconscious response to the above question.
- ☐ Act on this valuable information.
- ☐ List what people will say about you after you have lived your exceptional life. This points to your raison d'être.
- ☐ Act as if you know your purpose in life. Look the part—act the part.
- ☐ Go for your raison d'être without fear. Fear is simply a lack of faith in success. Fear is your worst enemy. Remove fear from your life.

Ask Yourself:

- ☐ What is important for me to know now?
- ☐ What is the most important thing I could do now to find my dream job?
- ☐ What would be my dream job?
- ☐ How can I find love in my life?
- ☐ What is my purpose in life?
- ☐ How can I make my life meaningful?
- ☐ What is the most important thing I can do now for my career?

Love

Chapter 3 for more detail.

- ☐ Nourish your self-esteem. Be a better tipper.
- ☐ Practice the affirmation: "I love myself."
- ☐ At the end of each day write down everything you did right and everything you would do differently next time.

- ☐ Stay away from people who erode your self-esteem.
- ☐ Love others and find others to love.
- ☐ Find people who enhance your life and who's lives you enhance. Cultivate those relationships.
- ☐ Create perfect friendships.
- ☐ Join with others to volunteer to make the world better.

Health—Our Responsibility

Chapter 4 for more detail.

- ☐ Find the "Truth" about health and how to be healthy. Don't leave it to your doctor or the ads on TV promoting pharmaceuticals.
- ☐ Cleanse your body inside and out of toxins.
- ☐ Use potassium balanced salt.
- ☐ Walk daily –think daily.
- ☐ Tap into the power inside yourself to heal and to become healthy.
- ☐ Eat Organic.
- ☐ Become knowledgeable on vitamin supplements. Use natural vitamins. Create a comprehensive supplement program.
- ☐ Use a sauna.
- ☐ Eat whole grains.
- ☐ Take minerals.
- ☐ Eat plain organic yogurt, kefir or buttermilk.
- ☐ Eat pollen-rich honey.
- ☐ Eat seaweed.
- ☐ Eat garlic.
- ☐ Research Chinese herbs.
- ☐ Find a doctor that is more interested in cures than in giving medication to cover up symptoms.
- ☐ Get enough sleep.

Appendix A
Your Exceptional Life Calendar

Wealth & Prosperity
Chapter 5 for more detail

☐ Get out of debt.

☐ Make a plan where your living expenses will be paid for by the surplus from your investments.

☐ Create a plan where you are completely free to use all 24 hours a day in any way you choose.

☐ Use your raison d'être to give power to your career, business, real estate and other investments.

☐ Make sure your head is on straight about making money. Do you love rich people?

☐ Become knowledgeable about the laws of money and risk. Learn from those who have had success.

☐ Buy tapes, CD's, books, and go to seminars on investing, prosperity and wealth.

☐ Create a synchronized plan for wealth and your raison d'être.

Goal Planning
Chapter 6 for more detail.

☐ Rank your career values.

☐ Rank your personal values.

☐ Reconcile both sets of values.

☐ Make a list of what you want in life—the longer the better. Answer why you want each item on the list.

☐ Make a list of what you want to avoid in life. Answer why you want to avoid each item on the list.

☐ Imagine living the perfect life and how that would feel.

☐ As you achieve each goal or item on the list, mark it "Exceptional Life."

- ☐ List the ten most important improvements for each area of your balanced life.
- ☐ Circle the three, in each area, that would have the most immediate impact on your life right now. Start your work on these goals today.

Truth

Chapter 7 for more detail.

- ☐ Find your current spiritual beliefs.
- ☐ Open your mind to all paths to truth.
- ☐ Read and research all religions, philosophy, and all great thinkers.
- ☐ Keep a diary or journal of your spiritual journey.
- ☐ Meditate, contemplate, and look for answers from within.
- ☐ Have fun with your search.

Mental Growth

Chapter 8 for more detail.

- ☐ Set up your health program to create a healthy brain.
- ☐ Create a designer brain with YOU being the intentional designer.
- ☐ Create a plan to manage your memories.
- ☐ Find your scotomas—find your blind spots.
- ☐ Program your subconscious by programming the small stuff.
- ☐ Face reality whether it is pain or joy.
- ☐ Find joy and happiness.
- ☐ Increase your enthusiasm.
- ☐ Eliminate all interruptions to your thinking.
- ☐ Create your own home library.

Appendix A
Your Exceptional Life Calendar

Legacy
Chapter 9 for more detail.

- ☐ Develop your children, spouse and friends to obtain their best potential. Help them to become their best selves.
- ☐ Find your raison d'être and purpose in life and you will leave a legacy.
- ☐ Take risks and make mistakes.
- ☐ Believe in prosperity and abundance.
- ☐ Create good memories for everyone whom you touch.
- ☐ Get out of the rut and into the groove.
- ☐ Use all relevant technology and tools to expand your powers for your raison d'être and legacy.
- ☐ Document your life with journals, pictures, tapes and video.
- ☐ For a true feeling of legacy, read the story *The Man Who Planted Trees* by Jean Gono and apply the lessons to your life.
- ☐ List the legacies you would like to leave. Make them part of your goals.

Continue
Chapter 10 for more detail.

- ☐ Move all obstacles from you life that will keep you from creating an exceptional life. Fear and procrastination are our biggest obstacles.
- ☐ Our raison d'être is the most important thing we can find out about ourselves. Dedicating our life to our purpose or raison d'être is more than half the battle to an exceptional life.
- ☐ One is lost until one loves. Everyone is searching for love. They would be better off if they just gave love without any

expectations, then they would have more love than they could handle.

☐ It is healthy to be responsible for one's health. Become your own health expert—it could save your life.

☐ Money and wealth are more in the mind than in the wallet. Create a wealth consciousness and the money will come.

☐ Use the most advanced computer on the planet to plan your life. Use your mind. Without goals and plans— nothing happens.

☐ Search out truth throughout your life. When you think you have the answers you may be more ignorant than your realize. Life is meant to be explored, sampled and experimented with every day. You are a witness to your life. What is your truth?

☐ If your mind is not growing then it is decaying. The greatest among us have grown their minds throughout their lives. That is why education is a lifelong practice.

☐ It could be that our legacy is our raison d'être. I know that most raison d'êtres leave a legacy. Use the power of legacy and what you will leave the world to energize your raison d'être.

INDEX

1

1+1=11, 110

A

A word of caution, 25
Actualized human being, 186
Adult onset diabetes, 51
Affirm Money or Affirm Our Purpose, 76
Africa, 201
Afterlife, 139
Agnostics, 124
Aimless Distraction, 164
Al Qaeda, 133
Alaska, 185
Aldonza, 130
Alexander the Great, 199
Allegory, 126
Allen, Woody, 71
Amazon.com, 184
Anakin Skywalker, 138
Analects, 141
Appleseed, Johnny, 189
Aquarian Conspiracy, The, 49
Arabian lamp, 112
Areas of wealth formation, 79
Armstrong, Lance, 4, 49
Arthritis, 55

Atheists, 124
Authentic self, 193

B

Babies, 29
Bach, Richard, 191
Balanced Life, 96
Barnum, Phineas Taylor, 71
Bartol, Cyrus A., 147
Bear Creek Farms, 7
Beatles, 39
Beethoven, 134
Beethoven, Ludwig Van, 4
Belief in Blessings or Curses, 72
Beliefs, 63
Bhagavad Gita, 140
Bible, James 2:26, 170
Bible, John 13:34, 28
Bible, Matthew 16:26, 94
Bible, Matthew 7:12, 142
Bible, Philippians 4:8, 110
Big Daddy, 194
Big fish, 85
Bingham, George Caleb, 135
Blessings, 178
Blind spots, 152
Blizzard, 83
Blog, 182
Bonfires of the vanities, 86

Bosque Eterno Do Los Ninòs, 175
Boss, 10, 32, 33, 85, 107, 109, 177
Bottom-up marketing, 183
Bouffier, Elzéeard, 189
Brain, 148
Brain re-wiring, 149
BRAVO, 197
Brick, 194
Broken heart, 29
Brothers, 202
Buddha, 140
Buffet, Warren, 137
Bulgarians, 66
Bull's eye, 11
Bulwer-Lytton, Edward, 147
Burns, Robert, 193
Buscaglia, Leo, 31, 191, 196, 203
Busse, Thomas, 156
Buy high--sell low, 73

C

Calcutta, 97
Canada, 77
Cancer, 77
Canfield, Jack, 110
Cardia Salt, 53
Career, 100
Career/Job or Business, 120
Carlyle, Thomas, 5
Carnegie, 187

Carnegie Hall, 149
Cat on a Hot Tin Roof, 195
Cave, 126
Celebrating Success—Or Failure, 196
Character, 85
Charles, Ray, 4
Chicken Soup for the Soul, 110
Child abuse, 33
Chinese, 68
Chinese herbs, 67
Chocolate, 27
Chorus, 132
Christopher Columbus, 153
Churchill, Winston, 6, 18, 19, 20, 200
CIA, 201
Cicero, 123
Circuit City, 200
Civil War, 185
Coca Cola, 165
Collins, Jim, 200
Columbia, Missouri, 41
Community, 117
Compassion, 23, 29, 37, 143, 201, 202
Compassionate Iris, 36
Confucius, 140
Congruent, 101
Contemplate, 145
Contrarians, 83
Cooley, Dick, 200
Copper, 56

Coué, Émile, 50
CPA, 83
Creating A Life Plan for Love, 42
Cure, 54

D

Danko, Dr. William, 78
Dark Ages, 86
Dark Side, 138
Darkened glass, 126
David, 86
Davis, Bette, 70
Declaration of Independence, 161
Deductions, 82
DeLay, Dorothy, 128
Delayed Dreams, 192
Dennis the Menace, 40
Descartes, Rene, 123
Despised, rejected and spat upon, 54
Detoxification, 56
Dhammapada, 140
Diabetes, 51
Diary, 14
DO NOT WANT, 106
Doctor Professor Longhair, 133
Dog, 6
Dogma, 136
Doing What We Can, 132
Don Quixote, 130
Don't Be Evil, 183

Don't tell your plans or you will dissipate your forces., 111
Double bind, 61, 74
Dr. Spock, 134
Dream house, 60
Dreams, 192
Dulcinea, 130
Dying from a lack of love, 30

E

Eat organic, 64
Ebay, 184
Edison, Thomas Alva, 13, 163
Einstein, Albert, 13, 163
Electric train, 105
Elephant, 72
Elvis, 133
Emerson, 154
Emerson, Ralph Waldo, 155
Employees, 9, 33, 34, 35, 76, 77, 86, 87, 94, 130, 136, 138, 158, 159, 181, 199
Enlightened manager, 86
Enron, 138
Enthusiasm, 162
Europe Through the Back Door, 92
Evil, 137
Expectations, 130
Exponential success, 111

F

Fadiman, Cliff, 171
Failure magnets, 73
Faith-Belief, 61
Fake it till you make it, 163
Fake love, 35
Family, 10, 24, 29, 31, 33, 34, 35, 39, 44, 45, 47, 51, 53, 54, 59, 65, 75, 77, 81, 82, 83, 95, 97, 102, 104, 109, 100, 101, 111, 115, 145, 172, 174, 178, 184, 187, 189
Fannie Mae, 200
Fasting, 57
Favorable stereotypes, 156
Feeling no emotional pain, 157
Ferguson, Marilyn, 49
Fifth stage of life, 173
Financial, 119
Financial calculator, 79
Financial freedom, 75
Find your heroes and you find yourself, 24
Finding balance in our goal planning, 94
Finland, 52
First Grade Teacher, 39
Focus on the positive, 108
Forbes, 136
Ford, Henry, 71
Fox, Terry, 77
France, 182, 189
Fraternal twins, 40
French, 60
Friends, Social, 116
Froogle, 53
Fruit of action, 32
Fuller, Buckminster, 163

G

Gain significance, 199
Gandhi, 1, 75, 123, 200
Garden, 37
Garlic, 67
Gates, Bill, 87, 133, 210
Genie, 112
Genius and life purpose, 12
Gifts, 22
Gillette, 200
GIMP, 55
Ginseng, 68
Goals, 76
Goethe, 48
Gold rush, 185
Golden Rule, 142
Gono, Jean, 189
Good or Bad, 176
Good to Great, 200
Google, 153, 183
Google Me, 182
Gotu Kola, 68
Grandparents, 105
Greek, 59, 126
Griffith, Andy, 91
Groove, 180
Group think, 137

H

Hamartia, 11
Handel, 134
Hansen, Mark Victor, 110
Happiness or Pleasure, 98
Happiness or raison d'être and quotations, 19
Harari, Herbert, 155
Harvard Business School, 136
Health, 121
Hear colors, 149
Heart disease, 51
Heaven and Hell, 139
Hell, 35
Heschel, Dr. Susannah, 133
Hidden blessing, 2
High blood pressure, 51
High Blood Pressure Solution, The, 53
Higher Reflection, 129
Higher Self, 137
Hillel, 141
Hindu, 140
Hippocrates, 56
Hubbard, Elbert Green, 147
Hula-Hoop, 155

I

I see God within you, 178
II conto, per favore, 197
Imbecile, 127
Impossible dream, 130
India, 97, 178
Indians, 153
Infinity, 94
Internet, 25, 53, 64, 79, 80, 81, 89, 127, 183, 185
Iodine, 67
IQ, 148
Iris, 36
Israel, 128
Italians, 60
Italy, 31, 92, 197

J

James, William, 164, 171
Japan, 67
Jesus, 142
Johnny, 196
journal, 21, 22, 24, 27, 44, 145, 161, 165, 166, 179, 185, 187, 188, 189, 194, 210, 214, 215
Journal of Educational Psychology, 156
Joy, 160
Juice bars, 58
Jung, Carl, 5, 191
Just good enough, 72
Just Over Broke, 79

K

Kamakawiwo'ole, Israel, 182
Keller, Helen, 49, 132
Kenya, 201
Kimberly-Clark, 200

King, Stephen, 191
Klondike, 185
Know thy self, 92

L

Lao-Tse, 141
Learned Helplessness, 16
Legacy, 186
Leprosy, 54
Let go and let God, 108
Lewis, C. S., 160
Li Chung Yun, 67
Library, 56, 111, 168, 186, 215
Library, 64
Lincoln, Abraham, 200
Lion, 201
Liszt, Franz, 149
Little Johnny, 196
Living Quickly--Slowly, 80
Living, Loving & Learning, 196
Lockstep, 128
Loose lips sink ships., 111
Loser, 73
love, 200, 202, 203
Love, 28
Love denied and Its Antidote, 37
Love your enemies, 37
Lucas, George, 137
Lymphatic system, 59

M

Macho, 201
Madison Avenue, 161
Make the Small Stuff-- Positive, 155
Making a Raison d'être Plan, 21
Making Your Balanced Goal Planning Life Plan, 112
Making Your Health Plan, 63
Making Your Life Plan in Search of Truth, 143
Making your wealth and prosperity plan, 88
Man of La Mancha, The, 130
Man Who Planted Trees, The, 189
Manifesting, 105
Marriage, Relationship, 115
Marx, Groucho, 42, 43
Masai, 201
Matterhorn, 108
Maxwell, David, 200
McDavid, John W., 155
Measure It, 103
Mechanical perfection, 128
Medical industrial complex, 51, 53
Meditate, 145
Meditation, 59, 125
Mehta, Zubin, 4
Memory strategy, 151
Mendacity, 194
Mental Growth, 118

Merchant of Venice, The, 36
Metechnikoff, Ilja, 66
Michelangelo, 6, 86
Microsoft, 87
Millionaire Next Door, The, 78
Minerals, 66
Missionaries, 31
Missouri, 7, 39, 41, 153
Mockler, Colman, 200
Monet, Claude, 135
Money, 75
Moore, Dr. Richard D., 53
Morrison, Marion, 155
Mother Teresa, 4, 30, 75, 97, 133, 200
Movie, 31
Muhammad, 141
Multi-tasking, 136
Murphy, Dr. Joseph, 63
Mystery of the Dark Side, 137

N

Namaste, 178
Name Stereotypes and Teachers' Expectations, 155
Nashville, 133
National Geographic, 67
National Public Radio, 143
Naturopath, 56
Negative stereotypes, 156
Neighbor lady, 37

New Age, 144
New York City, 60
Next evolutionary step, 149
No strings attached, 31
Norton Internet Security, 164

O

O'Connor, Johnson, 22
OK to be rich, 74
Once we make it, is pride an asset or a liability?, 85
Our First Legacy, 178

P

Pain, 53, 157
Pansalt, 53
Paramount importance, 93
Parental love, 39
Peale, Norman Vincent, 108
Pearls of wisdom, 1
People of lack, 72
Perfect Friends, 45
Perfect Spouse, 44
Peripatetic, 59
Perlman., Itzhak, 128
Personal, 101
Personal values, 102
Philosopher, 1, 48, 59, 123, 126, 140, 143, 144, 146, 147, 148, 186
Physician, 56
Pippi Longstockings, 40
Placebo, 61

Placebo affect, 62
Plain organic yogurt, 66
Plato, 126
Plotkin, Faith, 155
Poison pen, 151
Polar Express, 3
Pollen-rich honey, 66
Poor in love, 30
Poor in spirit, 30
Popcorn, Faith, 155
Potassium, 51
Poverty consciousness, 89
Power of Your
  Subconscious Mind,
  The, 63
Prayer, 61
Prescriptions, 68
Pride, 86
Principal's office, 40
Professional speaker, 198
Professor Bent, 34
Prosperity, 71, 74
Prosperity consciousness, 89
Protection Paradox—Fear
  or Confidence, 108
Provence, 189
Put on the shelf, 40

Q

Questions, 9
Qur'an, 141

R

Raison d'être, 93, 97

Ramsey, Dave, 90
Rauf, Imam Feisal Abdul, 133
Reflection, 59
Rembrandt, 135
Remen, Dr. Rachel
  Naomi, 101
Renaissance, 86
Resilient, 176
Respect, 33
Retire, 78
Rimsky-Korsakov, Nicolai, 149
Risk, 176
Risk taking, 2
Rock & Roll, 133
Rohn, Jim, 186
Roosevelt, Franklin D., 49
Rooster, 7
Rosa Ragosa, 65
Rose hips, 65
ROTH IRA, 79
Rudolph, Wilma, 4
Rut, 180
Rut or Groove, 180

S

Salem, MA, 185
Salt, 50
Samuel McIntire, 185
San Francisco, 60
Santa, 105
Sauna, 65
Savonarola, Girolamo, 86
Schuller, Robert, 130

Scotoma, 152
Scotoma—Our Blind
 Spots, 152
Scriabin, Alexander, 149
Sears, 105
Seattle, 7, 55
Seaweed, 67
Seize the day, 176
Self Esteem, 130
Self Love, 42
Self-sabotage, 16
Self-sufficient, 172
Seligman, Dr. Martin, 16
Selling short, 84
Shadows, 126
Shakespeare, William, 36, 124
Shaw, George Bernard, 176
Shayast-na-Shayast, 140
Ships, 153
Shock, 16
Should We Replace Emotion With Logic?, 133
Show me, 153
Simple Legacy, 185
Sleep, 69
Smith, Darwin, 200
Social capital, 35
Sodium, 51
Spiritual, 114
Stages of life, 172
Starship Enterprise, 134
Stereotypes, 153
Steves, Rick, 92

Strange Practices, 201
Stratton, George, 148
Strokes, 51
Subconscious, 13, 76, 103, 152, 157, 164, 165, 166, 208
Success to Significance, 198
Sugar Plum, 128
Supreme Court ruling, 14
Surprised by Joy, 160
Synchronicity, 77
Synchronized plan, 90
Synergistic synchronicity, 77
Synesthesia, 149

T

Tada, Joni Erickson, 4
T'ai Shang Kan Ying P'ien, 141
Taking the Bark Out of Dogma, 135
Talents, 22, 149, 165, 210
Talmud, 141
Taxes, 81
Temple University, 156
Tennessee Williams, 195
Tesla, Nikola, 14
Tharp, Twyla, 181, 182
The #1 Success Secret, 150
The Polar Express, 4
The Surprise of Small Daily Savings, 78
Think, 128

This I Believe., 143
Thyroid, 67
Tidal wave, 80
Time and money, 102
To Feel Loved, 32
Top-down marketing, 183
Torah, 141
Toxins, 57
Tracy, Brian, 91
Tsunami, 80
TV, 10, 11, 46, 60, 69, 94, 109, 127, 153, 164, 183, 212
Twain, Mark, 49, 206
Twins, 40

U

Uncle Nino, 31
University of Missouri, 34
University of Missouri Laboratory School, 41, 58
University of Sinkiang, 68
Unloving parents, 38
Upside-down, 148
Urban Renewal, 135
Use it or lose it, 148

V

Value people, 32
Value priorities, 102
Values, 100
Veracity, 196
Viagra, 165

Vincent Van Gogh, 28
Vitamin C, 65
Vitamin supplements, 68
Voltaire, 1, 148
Volunteer, 46, 212

W

Walgreen, Cork, 200
Walk, 58
Wall Street, 82, 83
Wallis, Reverend Jim, 133
War is Hell, 35
Washington, vi, 39
Washington, George, 200
Wayne, John, 155
Wealth, 71, 74
Weight Watchers®, 103
Wells Fargo, 200
What do I think, 129
Whole brain, 135
Whole grains, 65
Why Do Good Things Happen to Bad People?, 137
Williams, Tennessee, 195
Williamson, Marianne, 20
Winner, 72
Wright, 37
Wurtzel, Alan, 200

Z

Zig Ziglar, 10, 34
Zoroaster, 140

Help Others Have an Exceptional Life

Keep this book for your own library. Re-read the book until it is in your subconscious. Give additional books to all those people who deserve an Exceptional Life. Send it to both friends and enemies. Call your local library and make sure they have it in their collection. If not, donate the book on the condition that it will be put on the shelf.

See order sheet on the next page. Large orders receive a substantial discount. Call 800-745-6273 or email Orders@CranePress.com for quote.

Fast Order Form

Fax: 615-599-2018. Send this form.

Phone: 800-745-6273 Toll Free.

E-mail: Orders@CranePress.com

Snail Mail: Crane Press
    Order Department
    P.O. Box 680367
    Franklin, TN 37067

I would like to order the following books, tapes, cd's, or reports. I understand that I may return any of them for a full refund (less shipping costs and in original condition) within thirty (30) days after purchase.

_____
_____
_____

Please send me FREE information on:

☐ Other books   ☐ Speaking and Seminars   ☐ Consulting
☐ **Free Newsletter**

Name: _____
Address: _____
City: _____ State: ___ Zip: _____
Phone: _____
E-mail: _____

Sales Tax: Please add 9.25% for shipments to Tennessee.

Shipping: U.S.: $4.00 for first book or disk and $2.00 for each additional product.   **International:** $9.00 for first book or disk; estimated $5.00 for each additional product.

Payment: ☐ Cheque   ☐ Credit card:

☐ Visa   ☐ MasterCard   ☐ AMEX   ☐ Discover

Card number: _____

Name on card: _____ Exp. Date: _____

Signature: _____